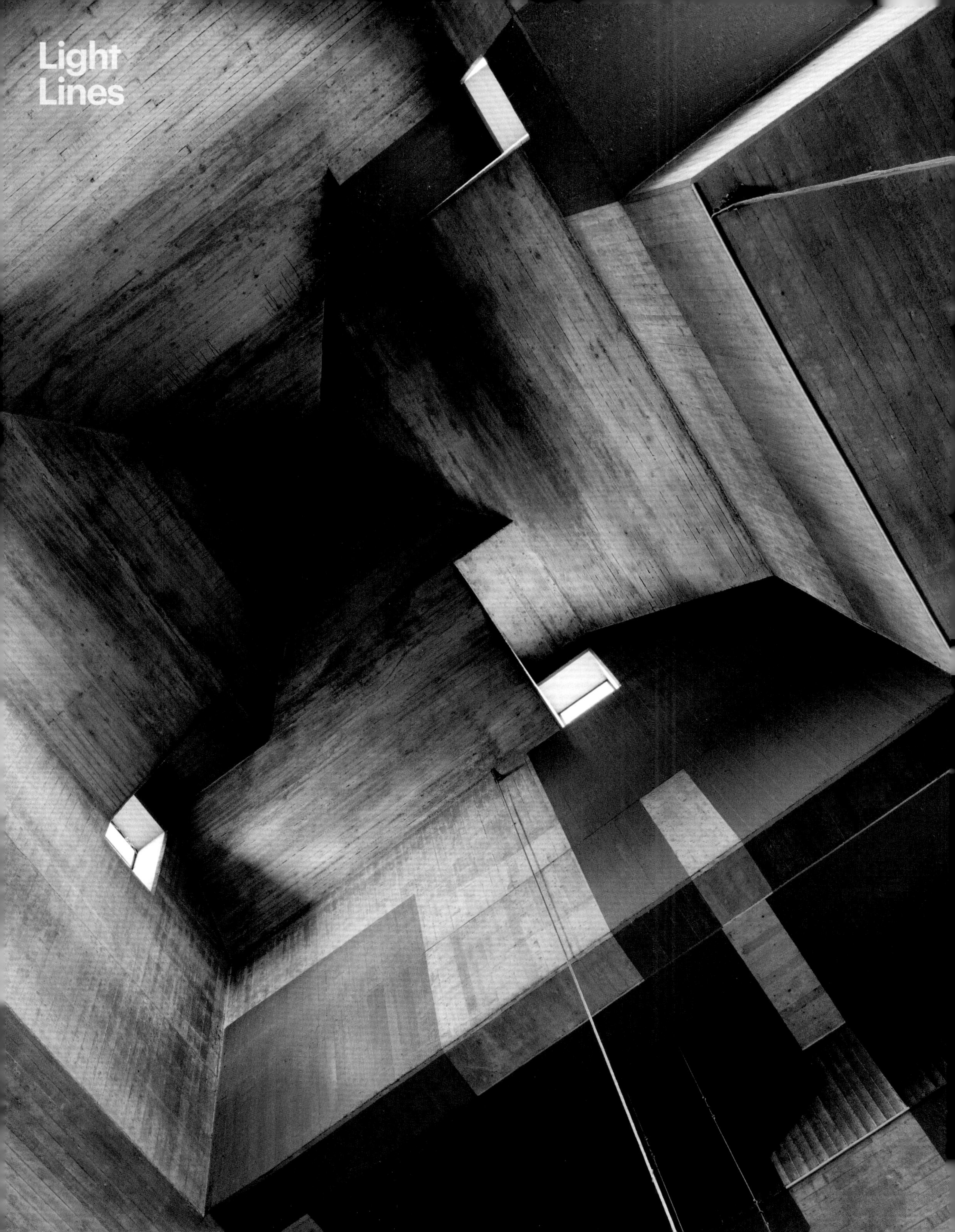
Light
Lines

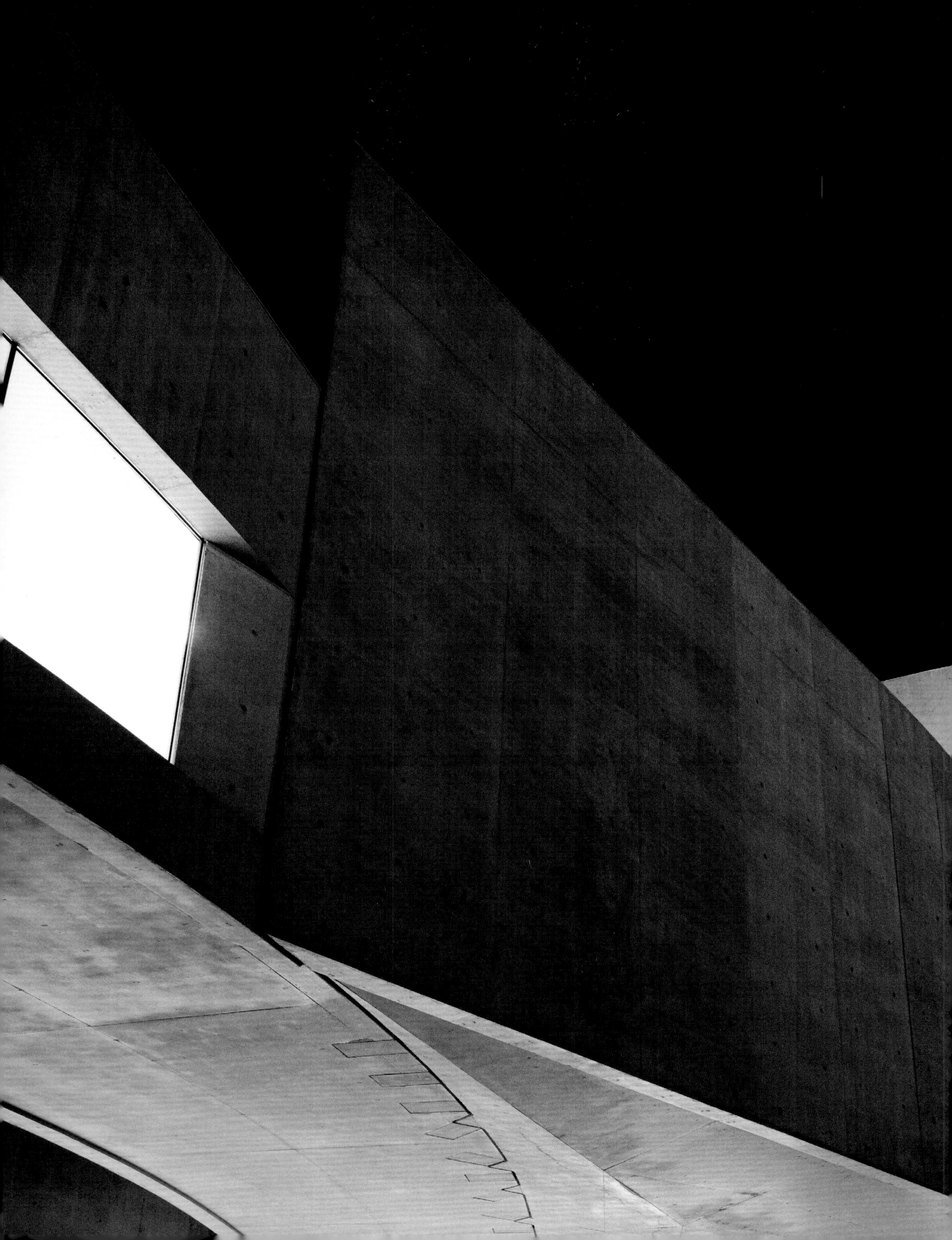

Light Lines

The Architectural Photographs of Hélène Binet

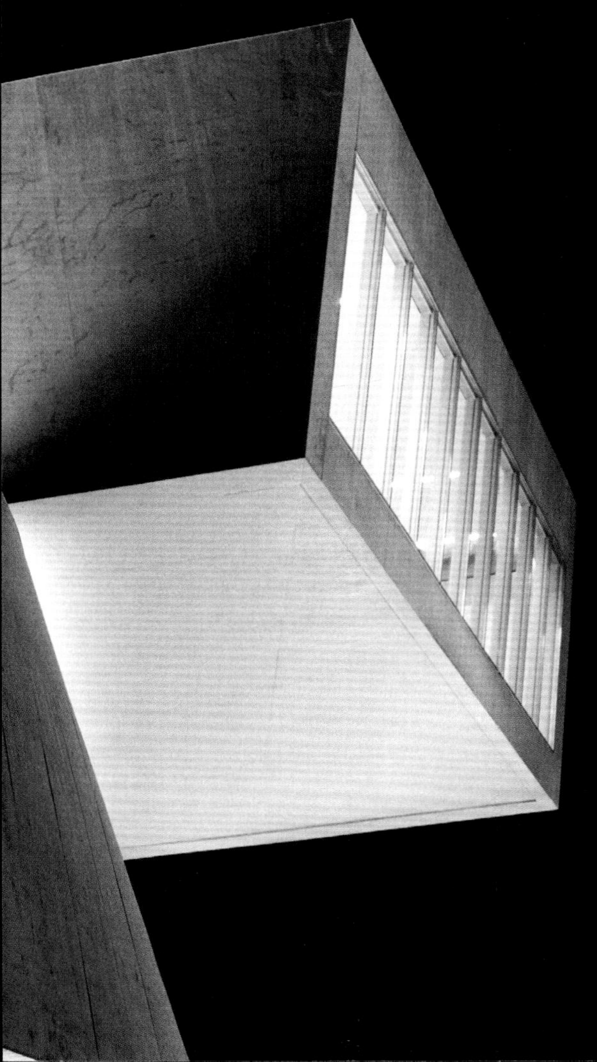

Royal Academy of Arts

First published on the occasion of the exhibition
'Light Lines: The Architectural Photographs of Hélène Binet'

Royal Academy of Arts, London
23 October 2021 – 23 January 2022

Supported by The Pictet Group and Pro Helvetia

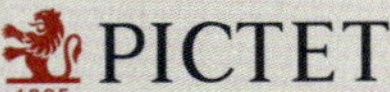 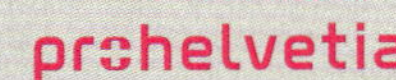

Exhibition curator
Vicky Richardson
with Rhiannon Hope

Exhibition organisation
Stephanie Bush
with Lucy Davis

**Photographic and copyright
co-ordination**
Susana Vázquez Fernández

Exhibition catalogue
Royal Academy Publications
Florence Dassonville, Production
and Distribution Co-ordinator
Carola Krueger, Production and
Distribution Manager
Peter Sawbridge, Head of Publishing
and Editorial Director

Copy-editing: Vicky Wilson
and Tom Neville
Design: JMG Studio
Colour origination and print:
Gomer Press, Wales

British Library Cataloguing-in-
Publication Data
A catalogue record for this book
is available from the British Library

ISBN 978-1-912520-85-5

Distributed outside the United States
and Canada by ACC Art Books Ltd,
Sandy Lane, Old Martlesham,
Woodbridge, Suffolk IP12 4SD

Distributed in the United States and
Canada by ARTBOOK | D.A.P., 75 Broad
Street, Suite 630, New York, NY 10004

Lender credits
Courtesy Large Glass, London: pages 23,
83, 93–5
Courtesy ammann // projects: pages 39,
43, 48–50, 57–69, 73–5, 78–9, 86–7, 90,
100, 103
Courtesy ammann // projects and Large
Glass, London: pages 40, 92
Courtesy Christian Bourdais: pages 70–1,
96–9
Private collection, courtesy Large Glass,
London: pages 88–9
The McGuinness Hooi Collection, courtesy
Large Glass, London: page 91

Photographic credits
All works are reproduced by kind
permission of the owners. Every attempt
has been made to trace the rights
holders of works reproduced. Specific
acknowledgments are as follows:
Unless otherwise stated, images of
all photographs are: © Hélène Binet
Page 12: © Jaroslav Zastoupil

Acknowledgments
The Royal Academy and Hélène Binet
would like to extend their deepest thanks
to the following individuals for their
support and involvement in realising this
exhibition: Kate Goodwin (who initiated
'Light Lines'), Gabrielle Ammann &
ammann // projects, Christian Bourdais,
Miguel Gonzalez, Adrian Locke, The
McGuinness Hooi Collection, Juhani
Pallasmaa, Martin Perrin, Charlotte
Schepke & Large Glass, Andrea Tarsia
and all who wish to remain anonymous.
In particular we would like to recognise
the efforts of Jasmine Bruno, assistant
to Hélène Binet, who has been integral
in the development of this exhibition and
accompanying catalogue, and Dirk Lellau
for his invaluable support in photographic
scanning and image editing.

Editorial note
All works are by Hélène Binet unless
otherwise stated.
Dimensions of all photographs are given
in centimetres, height before width.

Illustrations
Page 1: Gottfried Böhm, Church of
St Matthew, Düsseldorf, Germany,
2020. Courtesy ammann // projects
Pages 2–3: detail of page 59
Page 6: Le Corbusier, Couvent
Sainte-Marie de la Tourette, Eveux, France,
2002. Courtesy ammann // projects
Page 8: Daniel Libeskind / Studio
Libeskind, Jewish Museum, Berlin,
Germany, 1998

Contents

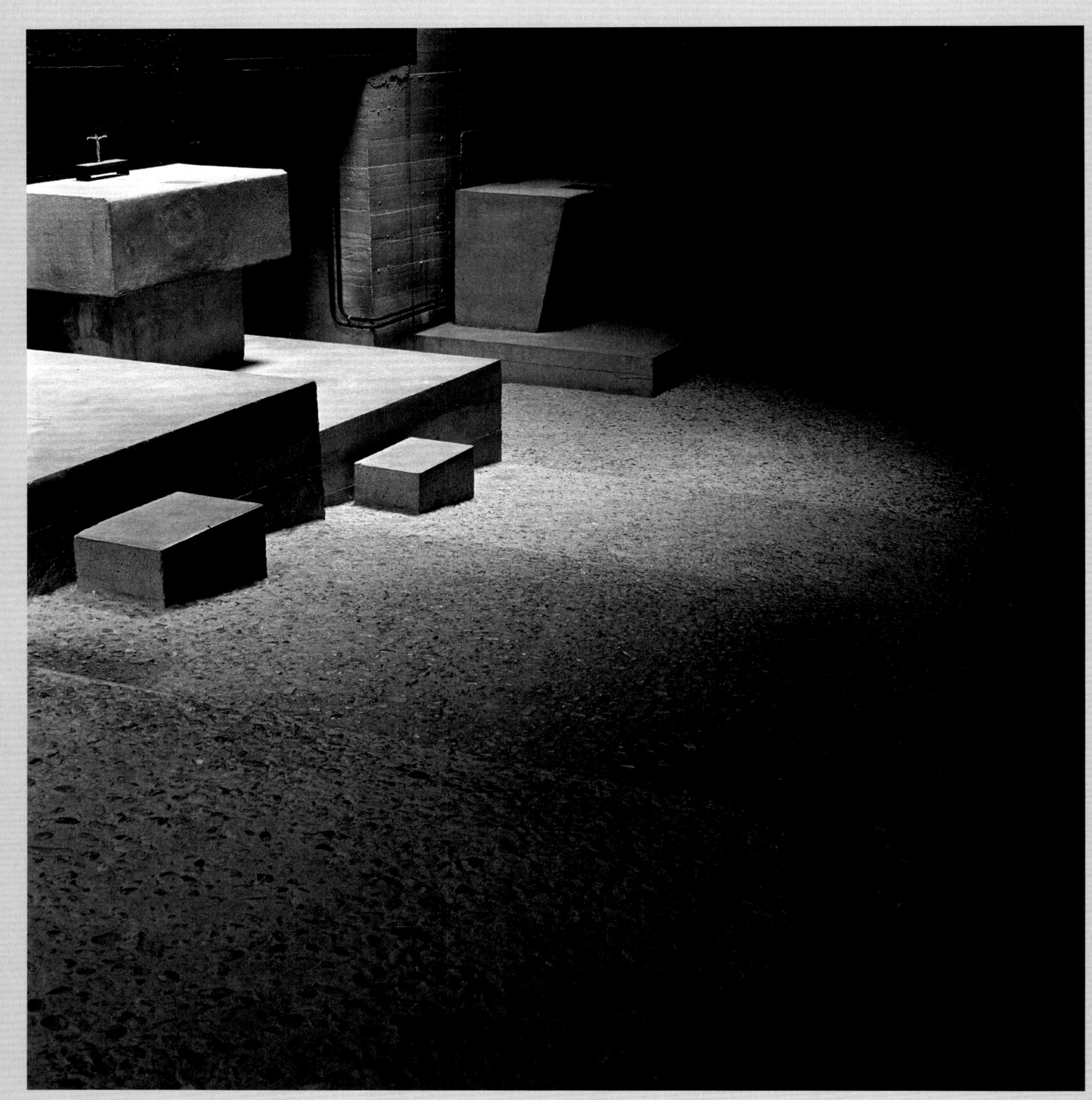

President's Foreword

We are delighted to welcome Hélène Binet back to the Royal Academy of Arts for her first major retrospective in the UK. Binet's photographs have been shown at the Royal Academy before: first in the 2008 Summer Exhibition, where her contribution won an Architecture Award, and again in 2014 when she made a powerful photographic essay of our exhibition 'Sensing Spaces'.

Over the past 35 years Binet has focused her practice on architecture. Under her gaze this rich subject has provided the framework for an exploration of light, shadow and space with her camera used as an instrument to ask questions about our place in the world. Since her first architectural photographs in the late 198Cs she has travelled to most parts of the globe, creating a body of work that speaks of the universal elements of architecture while being firmly anchored in time and place. She has developed a bond of respect and trust with many architects including the late Zaha Hadid RA, Daniel Libeskind Hon RA and Peter Zumthor Hon RA.

Binet is above all an artist. Her photographs make us think not just of abstract compositions but of poetry and music, reminding us that architecture has the power to move us emotionally and express ideas we cannot put into words.

'Light Lines' has grown from the exhibition 'Dialoghi', initiated in 2015 by the Academy of Architecture in Mendrisio, Switzerland. Our exhibition has evolved to include works from the entirety of Binet's career and to draw particular attention to her mastery of light, shadow and surface.

We are most grateful to Hélène Binet for allowing us to bring her work to the Royal Academy. We would also like to thank her assistant Jasmine Bruno, who has been a key member of the exhibition team alongside our staff. The exhibition, which was initiated by Kate Goodwin, has been expertly curated by our recently appointed Head of Architecture and Drue Heinz Curator Vicky Richardson and would not have been possible without the dedication of Stephanie Bush, Lucy Davis, Rhiannon Hope, Susana Vázquez Fernández and Miguel Gonzalez, as well as the creativity of Martin Perrin in his dual roles as exhibition and graphic designer. This beautiful book has been conceived and produced by RA Publications and designed by Jon Kielty. We are grateful to Juhani Pallasmaa for generously allowing us to reprint his eloquent essay.

Finally, we extend our deepest gratitude to our exhibition sponsors Pictet and Pro Helvetia for their generous support. We give additional thanks to the Swiss Embassy in London for their support of this exhibition.

Rebecca Salter PRA, President, Royal Academy of Arts

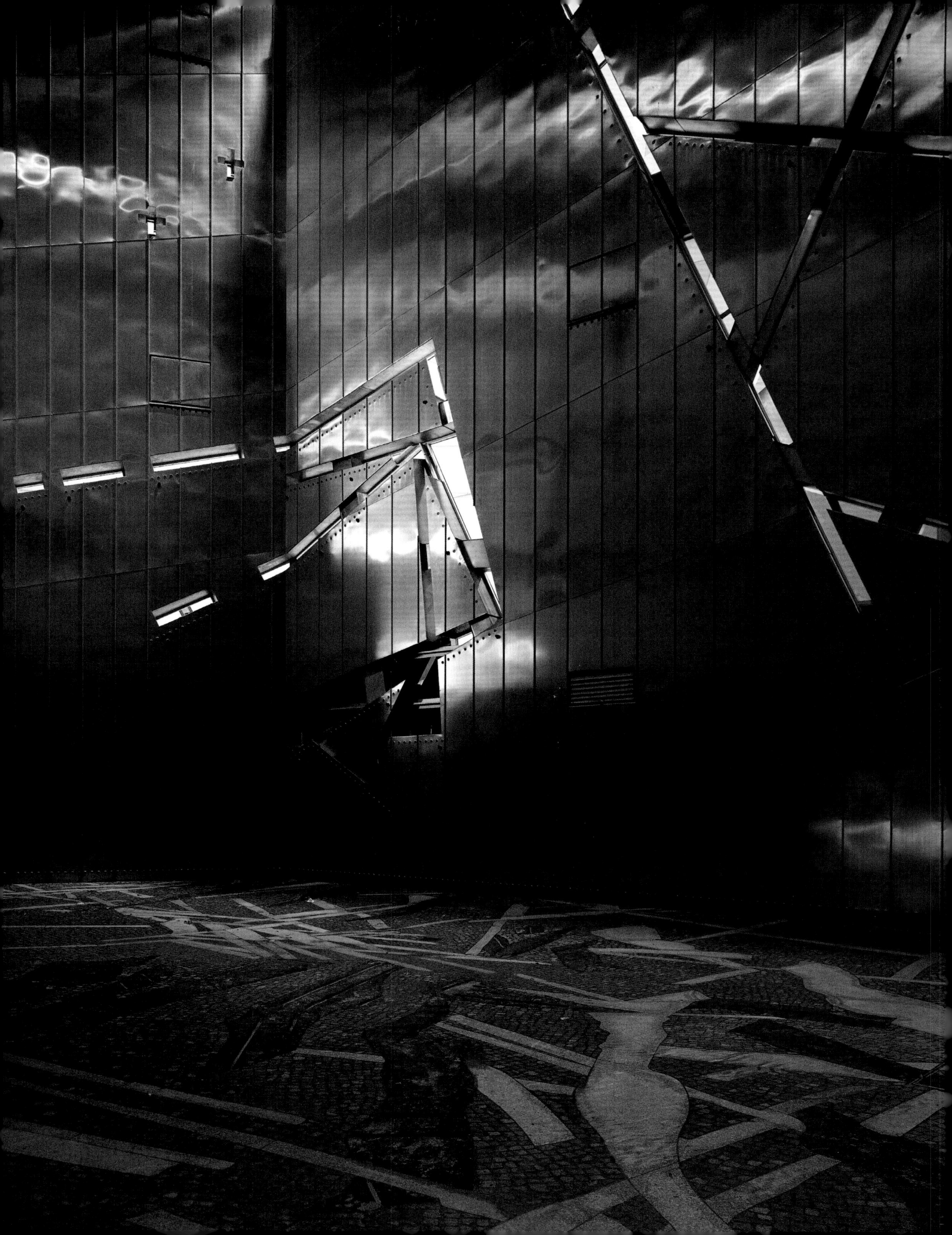

Alchemy of the Photograph
Juhani Pallasmaa

'A drawing of a tree shows, not a tree, but a tree-being-looked-at... Within the instant of the sight of a tree is established a life-experience,' John Berger writes in his book on drawing.[1] The same observation applies to the photograph. A photograph is often mistakenly seen as something more objective and 'real' than a drawing. Yet in both cases the image is bound to be an interpretative and constructed picture that oscillates between its two essences: a depiction of something out there in the world, and an intentional and imaginative image in its own right. Besides, every photograph and drawing is also a picture of its maker. And a great photograph depicts the world outside its frame, rendering simultaneously several realities and oscillating between them.

Architectural photography can be schematically divided into different approaches: the first aspires to record the architectural entity 'as it is', the second as it is confronted, selected, experienced and evaluated by the photographer, and the third uses the architectural subject as a material source to generate an independent abstracted image, a composition. Commissioned architectural photography usually aspires to follow the first approach. Hélène Binet's photographs of buildings are usually commissioned, but she does not intend to report on a building in its assumed objectivity or entirety. Her photographs are products of her individual and selective gaze, artistic intention and life experience. She does not attempt to record the architectural structure in its physical completeness or context. Instead, she aspires to convey the building's specific ambience and soul as experienced through her subjective perception and emotion.

Binet's photographs are most often fragments of buildings, or images of a passing phenomenon of light within their spaces or on their surfaces. Yet, enigmatically, they seem to portray the unifying spirit, the unique sense, of the architectural work. Alvar Aalto's muscular House of Culture in Helsinki is shown through an image of the concentric tile pattern of the entrance lobby or a piece of a delicately detailed handrail. Daniel Libeskind's dramatic and complex Jewish Museum in Berlin is shown through patches of daylight on a wall or floor.

Her photographs also pose intriguing questions about the relations of the viewed subject and the artistic intention, entity and detail, space and atmosphere, materiality and illumination, reality and image. Zaha Hadid's buildings turn into landscapes, while landscapes become intimate tactile surfaces as if they were the aged leather of a living creature. Even air tends to take on characteristics of solid matter; the sky is no longer a void, as it projects a sense of opacity and gravity. Her images accentuate materiality, as if they were intended to be experienced through the skin rather than the eyes. We are not usually aware of the fact that all our senses are modes of touching and originate in the skin. As Gaston Bachelard suggests: 'Matter is the unconscious of form,'[2] and: 'One cannot dream profoundly with objects. To dream profoundly, one must dream with substances.'[3] The material intensity of Binet's images projects a dreamlike reality, as if we were looking into something already forgotten or hearing a distant echo of the unseen reality hiding in the image.

Atmosphere is the complex immaterial, multi-sensory and relational synthesis of the experience of a spatial situation. 'I enter a room, and in a fraction of a second, have this feeling about it,' Peter Zumthor acknowledges.[4] It is the atmosphere, feeling or tuning that holds an architectural, literary, cinematic or musical entity together and gives it its sense of singularity, rather than any formal or geometric attributes. Hélène Binet seems to aim at conveying this very unifying ambience of the work rather than its material spaces or compositional configurations. The magic cohesion of atmosphere is akin to the mysterious quality of the holographic film, which can be cut into smaller and smaller fragments, yet each fragment contains the same full image. At each halving of the film, however, the viewing distance must also be halved in order to see the complete image again. Similarly, Binet's fragments magically contain the unifying feeling and authority of the whole, no matter how small they are.

The strong contrasts, deep shadows and forceful framing of her photographs bring to mind Lucien Hervé's famous images of Le Corbusier's works (or of the Jantar Mantar in Jaipur, which Binet has also photographed), whereas her capacity to tell a story through an extremely confined framing makes me think of Judith Turner's closely cropped architectural photographs. The tight framing of the subject also suggests the metaphysical world of miniatures in Giorgio Morandi's minute paintings. Both Morandi's paintings and Binet's photographs are intense meditations on the metaphysical question: Why do things exist rather than not? These are images that show 'the entire world reflected in a drop of water', as Andrey Tarkovsky described the cinematic approach of the film director.[5] A profound piece of art always contains more than its apparent subject-matter. Every true piece of art is a universe and, consequently, experientially endless. The protagonist of Michelangelo Antonioni's last film, *Par-delà les nuages* (1995), a photographer (portrayed by John Malkovich), expresses the complexity and enigma of artistic imagery at the very end of the film: 'But we know that behind every image revealed, there is another image more faithful to reality, and in back of that image there is another, and yet another behind the last one, and so on, up to the true image of the absolutely mysterious reality that no-one will ever see.'

Binet rarely uses colour and when she does, its intensity as well as the three-dimensionality of the depicted space are decisively reduced. Sometimes the colour has been suppressed to the point that it takes a while to realise that you are actually looking at a colour photograph. In her pictures of Zumthor's Therme Vals, the colour unifies space, matter and light. Stone and water fuse into a singular substance with a deep inner glow, as if the light emanated from matter rather than an ordinary source of illumination.

The materials in her images seem to be the results of a metamorphosis. In the images of Zumthor's thermal baths, water acquires an authoritative intensity and weight, as if it were liquid stone, whereas the ruffled dark cavity of his Bruder Klaus Field Chapel conveys the smell of smoke and lead; this is in fact dark light. The dark red bricks of Sigurd Lewerentz's St Mark's Church obtain a flesh-like sensuality and converse with the bark of the birch trees around, whereas the stone fragments of Dimitris Pikionis's pathways to the Parthenon suggest a dramatic and epic narrative, like the linguistic fragments of James Joyce, or another scale and distance, as in the immense earth drawings at Nazca. John Hejduk's housing and architectural sculptures seem to conceal a secret, as they exude an unidentifiable threat, while the countless concrete blocks in Peter Eisenman's Holocaust memorial in Berlin project the panic of suffocation and being eternally lost. The cobbled pavement of Caruso St John's square in Kalmar turns into an experience of hearing, as the photograph makes one imagine walking across the uneven pavement and hearing one's own footsteps bouncing off the boundary walls of the space. But senses want to collaborate and exchange the information they have gathered. The occasional shadows on the stones suggest an air of drama, movement and fatality, akin to the unforgettable scenes in Ingmar Bergman's films.

The world seen in Hélène Binet's cropped close-ups is an intense, intimate and private world for the viewer alone. The viewer senses the pulse of reality.

1   John Berger, *Berger on Drawing*,
    Jim Savage (ed.), Aghabullogue,
    Co. Cork, 2007, page 3.
2   *Gaston Bachelard: On Poetic
    Imagination and Reverie*, selected,
    translated and introduced by Colette
    Gaudin, Dallas, 1987, page liii.
3   Gaston Bachelard, *Water and Dreams:
    An Essay on the Imagination of Matter*,
    Dallas, 1982, page 22.
4   Peter Zumthor, *Atmospheres
    – Architectural Environments –
    Surrounding Objects*, Basel, Boston
    and Berlin, 2006, page 13.
5   Andrey Tarkovsky, *Sculpting in Time*,
    London, 1986, page 100.

Hélène Binet in Conversation with Vicky Richardson

Vicky Richardson: Architecture has been the major theme of your work since the beginning of your career. Where did your interest come from?

Hélène Binet: I grew up in Rome in the 1960s and this must have influenced the development of my sensibility. I was educated at home and had a lot of free time for projects that weren't part of a normal curriculum. Later on, in the 1980s, John Hejduk and Daniel Libeskind were the first architects to have an impact on me – through them I discovered that the process of making architecture can be extremely deep and poetic.

VR: Can you tell me a little about your family?

HB: They are all musicians: my parents, my grandfather, my brothers and my sister. Growing up I had a lot of ideas and intuition, but I couldn't express them academically, or in music or dance. Discovering photography was a revelation. I finally felt that my thinking and making were flourishing together.

VR: So after studying photography in Rome you came to London in the mid-1980s?

HB: Yes. Raoul Bunschoten, who later became my husband, was teaching at the Architectural Association. I was very inquisitive and it was a vibrant time for architecture. Raoul was working with Hejduk to build The Collapse of Time (1986), a temporary structure in Bedford Square outside the AA. I'd never seen anything like it. It was a project that examined the possibility of creating a work that is both medieval and modern, about time and the role of monuments. As David Shapiro wrote in his introduction to the book that contained my photographs of the work: 'it is Hejduk's idiosyncratic blending of private and public space that has permitted him to make, at once, something as portable as a timepiece into something as monumental as an obelisk.'

But at that time I wouldn't say I was driven by architecture itself. I was probably frustrated with the education I'd received in Rome, which was very technical and skewed towards advertising. My own interest lay in how to express ideas with my camera: it was a tool with which to question the world and photographing architecture gave me the chance to do that.

VR: It seems that the architects and clients you had in those early days are still very important to you.

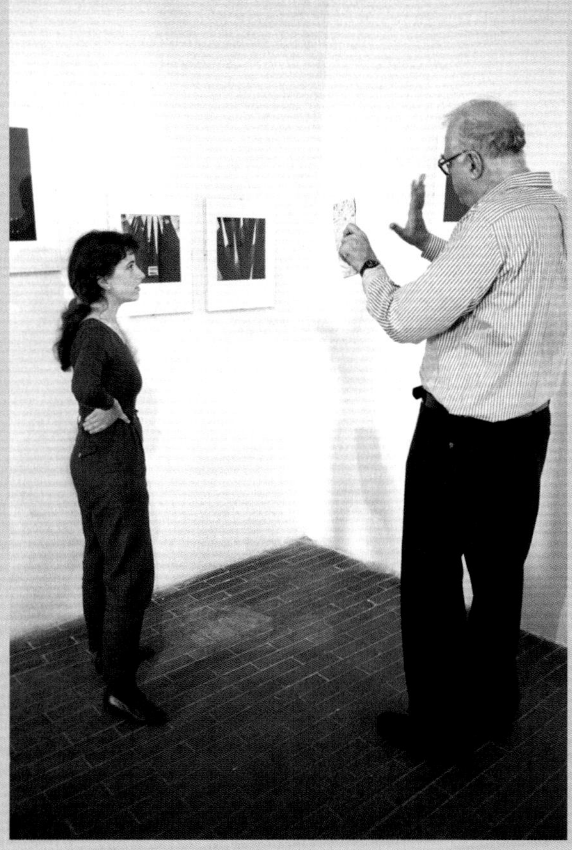

Hélène Binet and John Hejduk, photographed in 1990 by Jaroslav Zastoupil at the Galerie Jaroslav Fragnera in Prague during the exhibition 'Relatives: Complete Works of John Hejduk'

HB: Yes, I still carry with me the importance of those formative years, thanks to the wonderful architects I met and to Alvin Boyarksy, Chairman of the AA. Alvin was passionate about books and photography. In 1989 he sent me first to Sweden to photograph buildings by Sigurd Lewerentz and then to Greece to photograph Dimitris Pikionis's landscape at the Acropolis.

VR: Your first architectural photographs were of Hejduk's IBA housing in Kreuzberg (1988). What was it like to be in Berlin a year before the Wall came down?
HB: It was a unique experience to be in that still-divided city, suffering from its war-wounds. Artists, film-makers and writers have all reacted to that darkness. But while there was a dark atmosphere, it was open, and this must have been very relevant for Hejduk. A bomb site is full of pain, but it is also a *terrain vague* with its invitation to possible innovative interventions.

The housing scheme was Hejduk's first building. I had never photographed a building before, and I had to ensure that a simple shot could convey the depth of the work. The question of language in photography is very important: at that time mine was quite intuitive but later on I realised that I was laying the foundations for my way of conveying meaning within an image. Black and white, details, unfolding a second hidden layer, framing in a way that the image is a complete world; all of these are still part of my vocabulary when I photograph.

VR: How did your photographs of Daniel Libeskind's work come about?
HB: I've never had a commission from Libeskind: all my photographs of his work I initiated myself, with his blessing. In the mid-1980s I photographed symbolic projects such as The Machines (1985) and the House without Walls (1986). A decade later, in 1996, I photographed the Jewish Museum under construction. I was on a short visit to Berlin and Nina, Daniel's wife, explained that the building site would be closed at the weekend, but told me where I could jump over the fence. So those photographs were made in an intense afternoon.

VR: Did you feel the sense of emotion in the project?
HB: I knew about the void and the importance of the lines – I knew that every window is connected with an area in the city in which a Jewish family was murdered. I remember Libeskind's words: 'The new extension of the museum is conceived as an emblem where the not visible has made itself apparent as a void, an invisible.' But the impact was so unsettling and the responsibility of translating this into a photographic image was a challenge. Black is often associated with absence and light with life – but in this case I had to use the light as a way to get close to the invisible, with the black to frame it.

VR: Another key architect for you emerged in that period. You took an amazing set of photographs of Zaha Hadid's Vitra Fire Station at Weil am Rhein, both during construction and soon after it was completed in 1993.
HB: I remember the collective joy and excitement at the AA when she was completing her first building. When the invitation came – through Signy Svalastoga, who worked on the project – to photograph the building site, it was a dream come true. Why did I love photographing building sites and concrete so much? I still don't know. Is it the idea of working with a unique moment? Telling the story of a building's making? Or disclosing how Zaha was trying to defeat gravity with her canopy with its elegant constructivist energy?

I used a 4 × 5 camera that had been lent to me by Dennis Crompton, one of the founders of Archigram and head of the Communications Unit at the AA. He lent me the camera, the film-holders and the lenses. I also had a Hasselblad, which I've always used. I like to have two formats: 6 × 6 is very playful and there is no hierarchy, which is not the case with the 4 × 5 camera where the horizontal and vertical have very different narratives. A 6 × 6 is not as practical for photographing architecture or describing the structure of a building but it enables one to catch the little phenomena that light creates within places. In the case of the Vitra Fire Station the square format allowed me freedom with the composition to get close to Zaha's drawings and energy. After that, there were always commissions from Zaha: it was the beginning of a long collaboration.

VR: How did these collaborations work? Did she give you instructions and ask you to capture particular things?
HB: She would be short and direct. And then she would say funny things: 'Make it sexy', 'Don't forget to lie on the floor to capture it from beneath', 'Use your best lens!'. She was playful and didn't want to instruct me too much.

We shared a passion for building sites. As her buildings had already been widely photographed, I had the artistic freedom to make a photograph and not a representation of a building, and I'm so glad she gave me this opportunity.

VR: How did your conversation about the Ponte sul Basento, designed by Italian engineer Sergio Musmeci in the late 1960s, come about?
HB: The commission to photograph the bridge came from my friend, architect and curator Victor Jones, whom I met in Los Angeles. When the photographs were done, I heard that Zaha had been very inspired by the bridge. Woody Yao, Director of Zaha Hadid Design, told me that she'd said it would be lovely to have my photographs of the bridge on show alongside her work. But then, sadly, she passed away and there hasn't been the opportunity until now.

Both architects' works have in common the attempt to defy gravity and an interest in new technology and experimental form. Apparently Musmeci used only handwritten calculations and simple handmade models to design his bridge's structure. The two share an aesthetic, particularly Zaha's later aesthetic, when her work became more about curves.

VR: You speak with a lot of passion for Hadid's work, but your photographs for Peter Zumthor have been an equally important part of your career. How do you compare these experiences?
HB: Zaha's work was more difficult to frame than Zumthor's. At her Heydar Aliyev Center in Baku, for instance, it's like trying to control an erupting volcano – you see all these free curves and there's always a sense that by going a bit further you'll get a better photo. With Zumthor, you arrive in Vals, you see the baths, you see the lines, you see the walls. It's all there, no need to go any further. It's very calming and the decisions are more natural than in a building that is already so overwhelming.

VR: You've photographed many of Zumthor's buildings over the past 25 years and you have published several books together. The thermal baths at Vals was the first project by Zumthor that you photographed. How did that come about?
HB: I started to work with him in 1996, the year Therme Vals was completed, but I barely knew who he was then. I had seen an exhibition at the AA of his work photographed by Hans Danuser. The work we started together was a monograph, published by Lars Müller. Zumthor was not interested in being widely published, but he did want to make a book that would reflect the nature of his architecture.

VR: How did you find meeting him and going to his studio?
HB: We almost never talked about architecture. He said, 'Please don't ask me to show you my buildings.' Instead we'd go for walks, listen to music or talk about the format of the books. He was very open about how I should photograph the baths. I remember at one point he said, 'You have to remember that it's a place for the body to feel well, and you have to have that in your photograph.' But that was all.

VR: You've said that in the early part of your career you worked intuitively, using the camera as a means to try to understand the world. When did you begin to have the confidence that comes across so strongly in your work?
HB: I have always been confident within my work, but I started to formulate my decision-making when I was asked to give my first lecture and I began to define my perception of space within photography. I've felt the limitation of the camera in representing architecture: there's no way you can describe everything that belongs to the experience of space. It was clear to me that I was creating photographs that work because they contain their own world and don't try to capture the architecture in its totality.

VR: Do you mean that you felt overwhelmed by the amount of information and ideas?
HB: Not exactly. Space isn't only a visual experience, it's something that we perceive with all our senses: for example, we might feel warm and comfortable, or notice a particular aroma or smell, or recall memories of a previous visit. Yet with space, somehow, sight still seems to be the dominant sense. I think it was Leonardo da Vinci who said the eye is 'the window of the soul'. Of course, as photographers, we have to celebrate the visual, but it is important to understand where our experiences are coming from and which techniques to use to capture them within two dimensions. Photography can do something that architecture cannot: it can be displaced; it can be brought together on a wall in an exhibition or on the pages of a book. This allows combinations of images to be made; it's a very specific art. This dialogue is imaginary and personal, giving readers the chance to create their own new space.

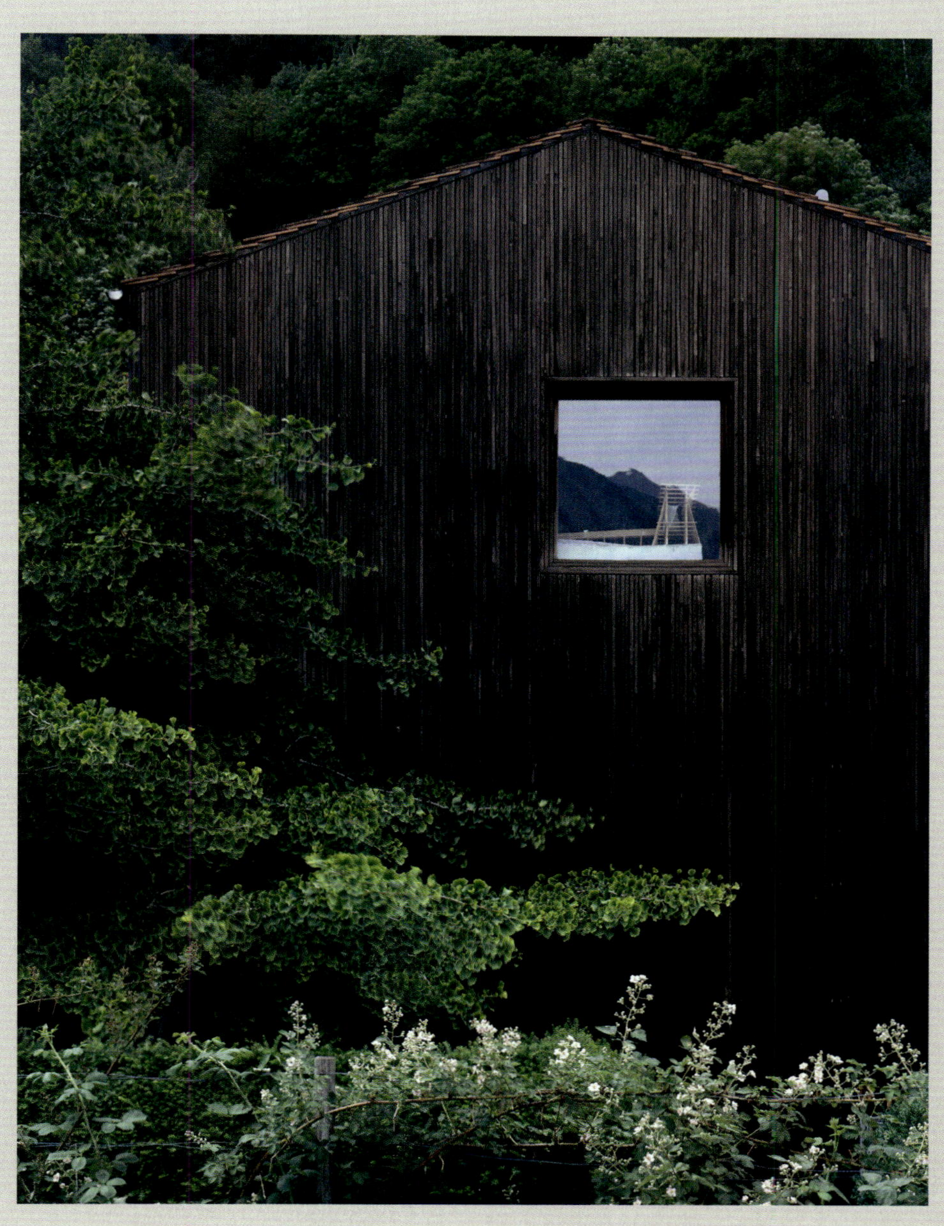

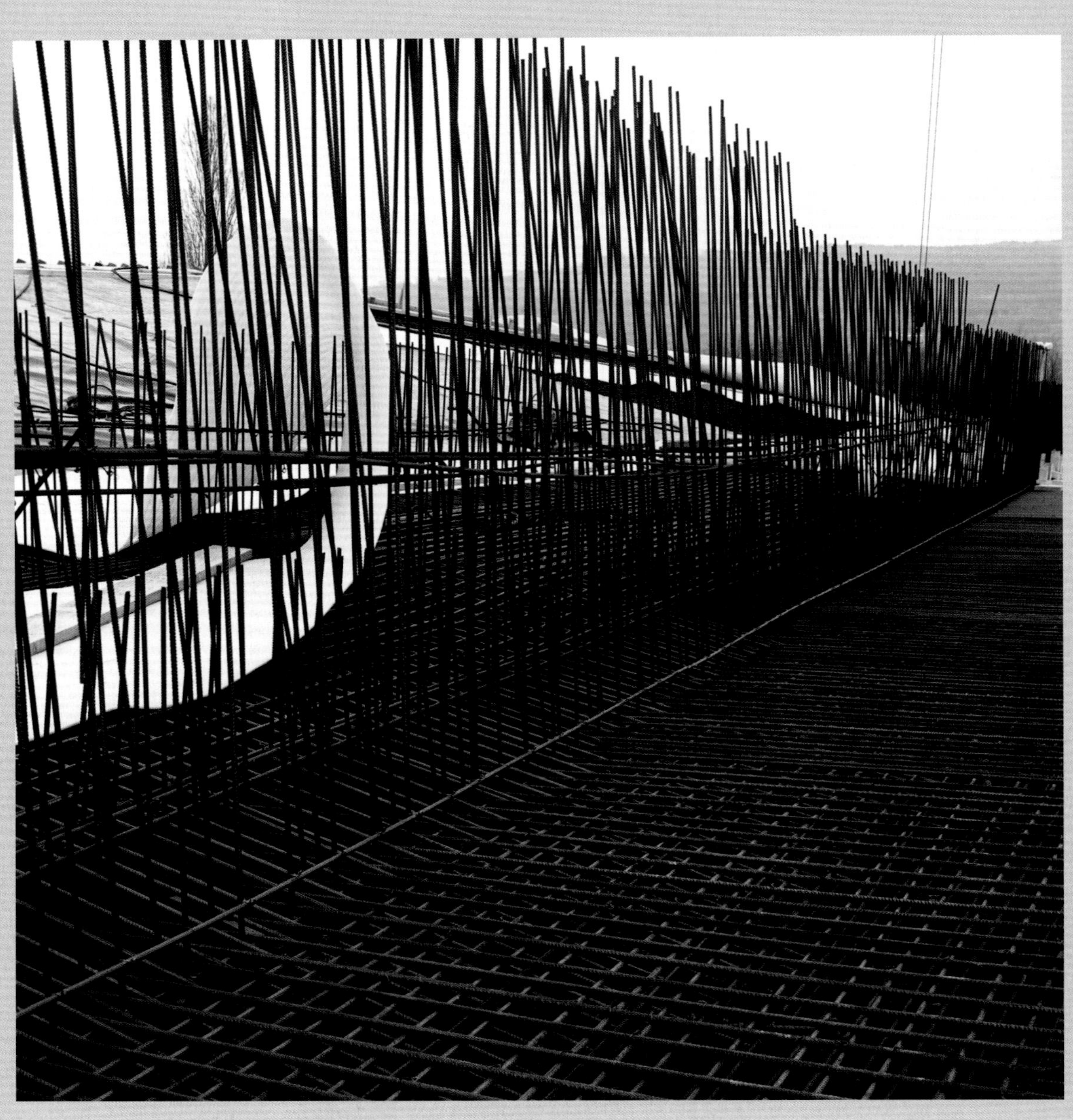

VR: Is this why you've limited yourself mostly to the use of black and white?

HB: I've always tried to get to the essence of a space, partly as a reaction to the feeling in the architectural profession that photography should do more – wider angles, more colour, more technique, and these days, Photoshop. Given the impossibility of representing architecture itself, the tendency can be to overdo it, whereas my strategy is to withdraw. Reducing the image to black and white is somehow more powerful. Aristotle said we can hear better in darkness. If I make a reduced image, you can feel it more. With a detail I'm going to tell you one thing about the building – a crack in a wall, the way a stair is made – so that you enter, you perceive, you feel it and you take it with you.

In the cinema there is this beautiful tradition of the illusion, a wonderful gift that I felt recently while watching *Cinema Paradiso* (1988). And my question is: is architectural photography part of this tradition? Could architectural photographs act like magic lanterns, transporting you away from the ordinary? In photography, the concept of space is almost scary; only a bit of magic can take it away.

I was influenced by reading Gaston Bachelard's *The Poetics of Space* (1958). He said that memory is anchored in space, not in time and history. I loved the word 'anchor' and I always think of a boat sailing away with our memories.

VR: The relationship between architecture and light is a recurring theme in your work, particularly the way that light enters the interior from outside, which seems very striking in lots of projects. Are you looking for that when you photograph a building?

HB: That touches on a very important point. I've always been mesmerised by the potential of light. In my work, the link between light and architecture is particularly important because I am fascinated by the fact that you cannot understand the quality of light without a body to receive it, and you cannot understand this body without the light that touches it. This duality is at the core of my photographs of space.

In 2002, for the exhibition 'The Secret of the Shadow: Light and Shadow in Architecture' at the Deutsches Architekturmuseum in Frankfurt, I was commissioned to photograph Le Corbusier's Couvent Sainte-Marie de la Tourette near Lyon and the Jantar Mantar Observatory at Jaipur. At that point I started to look more into the history of shadows and light. I tried to understand in a more poetic way the meaning of a shadow – maybe in the beginning there was darkness, before light came, so basically every time you interact with darkness you are connected in time and space and their sublime dimensions. My interest in space and light was driven by their capacity for giving shape to a dimension that is otherwise hard to grasp.

VR: Although you said earlier that you couldn't express your ideas in music, you make a comparison between light and music in architecture. How is music important in your work?

HB: I usually use analogies with music to explain how I work. Just like shadows, silence is an absence of energy. Moments of silence are very important in the structure of a piece of music: they demarcate the beginning and end and give a tempo. Blackness and shadows play the same role in creating a beginning and an end, in structuring a composition and giving it a tempo.

At La Tourette I encountered the celebrated beautiful corridor, with its very large clear-glass window with many irregular horizontal and vertical glazing bars that was designed by Iannis Xenakis, who began his career as an architect but became a composer. The window has been discussed as if it were a piece of music, and it almost has a harmony and counterpoint – you can read it horizontally, but you can also read it vertically. I photographed some of the window as it is, but what I was really interested in is what it *does*. So I started to photograph the floor with the lines of light coming from the window. Because two corridors intersect there, the lines started to mix and interfere with each other. Observing them, I began to think that these are almost dissonances, as in the music of Xenakis. When you look at a window with many glazing bars and you stand sideways, you notice a tiny beam of light; with my Hasselblad I followed the sun's movements and then bit by bit the bars opened up. Similarly, on the ground, the beams of light opened up as the sun became more perpendicular to the window.

VR: So you were thinking of the building and your camera as if they were musical instruments?

HB: In that case, absolutely: the music was the light. And

in addition, I was photographing Xenakis's architecture as if it were an orchestra.

VR: I wonder why you don't usually include people in your photographs: the Jantar Mantar Observatory is one of the few examples?
HB: The reason is that I want *you* to go into the photograph. If I include a person you immediately start to reflect on the role of that person. I made one of the images of the observatory with people because it's about marking the presence on Earth of people looking at the light.

Photographers such as Lucien Hervé and Henri Cartier-Bresson have made amazing pictures of space and people, so it's not impossible, but it dates the images very much and they become specific moments in a story. In the industry there's an idea that if you photograph a building with people in it, then it's the proof of a better piece of architecture.

VR: What took you to India?
HB: After photographing La Tourette for 'The Secret of the Shadow' it was very hard to find another building that had the same range of shadows. I decided to take a structure that makes shadows meaningful, because of culture or religion, as a way of understanding who we are. I imagine that Le Corbusier had seen the Jantar Mantar and had loved it, so I had a good combination of reasons to go there. The name Jantar Mantar is derived from the Sanskrit origins of *yantra* (instrument) and *mantra* (a spiritual and cultural guideline in Hinduism based on astrology). The Jantar Mantar was built at the beginning of the eighteenth century, around the time of Hawksmoor's London churches, which I was commissioned to photograph by Mohsen Mostafavi for the 2012 Venice Architecture Biennale. Mohsen had an idea that the towers of the churches were designed to be visible from the Thames and be used in navigation by passing ships. So I think it's quite interesting that Hawksmoor's churches are doing something similar to the observatory at around the same time, although on a completely different scale and in a different country.

VR: Could you say something about the series of photographs you took of Gottfried Böhm's churches to celebrate his centenary in 2020?
HB: Böhm's churches are distinctive. Unlike classical churches they don't have an established path; instead, they encourage visitors to find their own. Each corner, detail, texture and moment of light or colour inspires the viewer to have their own experience. That was one of the key readings of Böhm's architecture for me – that you can find your own little corner with your own god and your own soul. I think he deals with this desire in a very beautiful way.

VR: As well as looking up to see light in a space, you often use the ground to reveal the traces of use over time and walls to frame a view. When did you first start to become interested in these elements of architecture?
HB: I photographed Pikionis's paths at the Acropolis very early in my career, and that project helped me to develop a sensibility for what happens when places have been used by people over many centuries. In steps, on walls and on the ground, we can feel the presence of past generations.

When I went to Jørn Utzon's house, Can Lis in Mallorca, and to China to make a photographic essay of the Classical Gardens of Suzhou, I was trying to imagine a landscape or the horizon by looking at the walls. I wanted to push observers to look beyond what they see. My photographs of walls are a move towards the most abstract point of photographing architectural space. The moment you are limited by a wall, you start to imagine what is behind it.

VR: How important is it for you to study the work of architects or the background of a building before you take photographs of it?
HB: We talked about music, and I think I always have the architect's score in my mind, with its specific period and style. I hope that my interpretation is distinctive, but of course the score is always by the architect. To date, it's been a very enriching story. It's a way of working where I feel I get back what I give all the time.

VR: You say 'to date'. Does that mean that you might take a different direction in the future?
HB: My intention is not to leave architecture, but to keep exploring the subject more widely, whether to look at silence in architecture or transitional space in different cultures. I would like to photograph these topics and observe how they manifest themselves in specific buildings and how they can be translated into photography.

Catalogue Plates

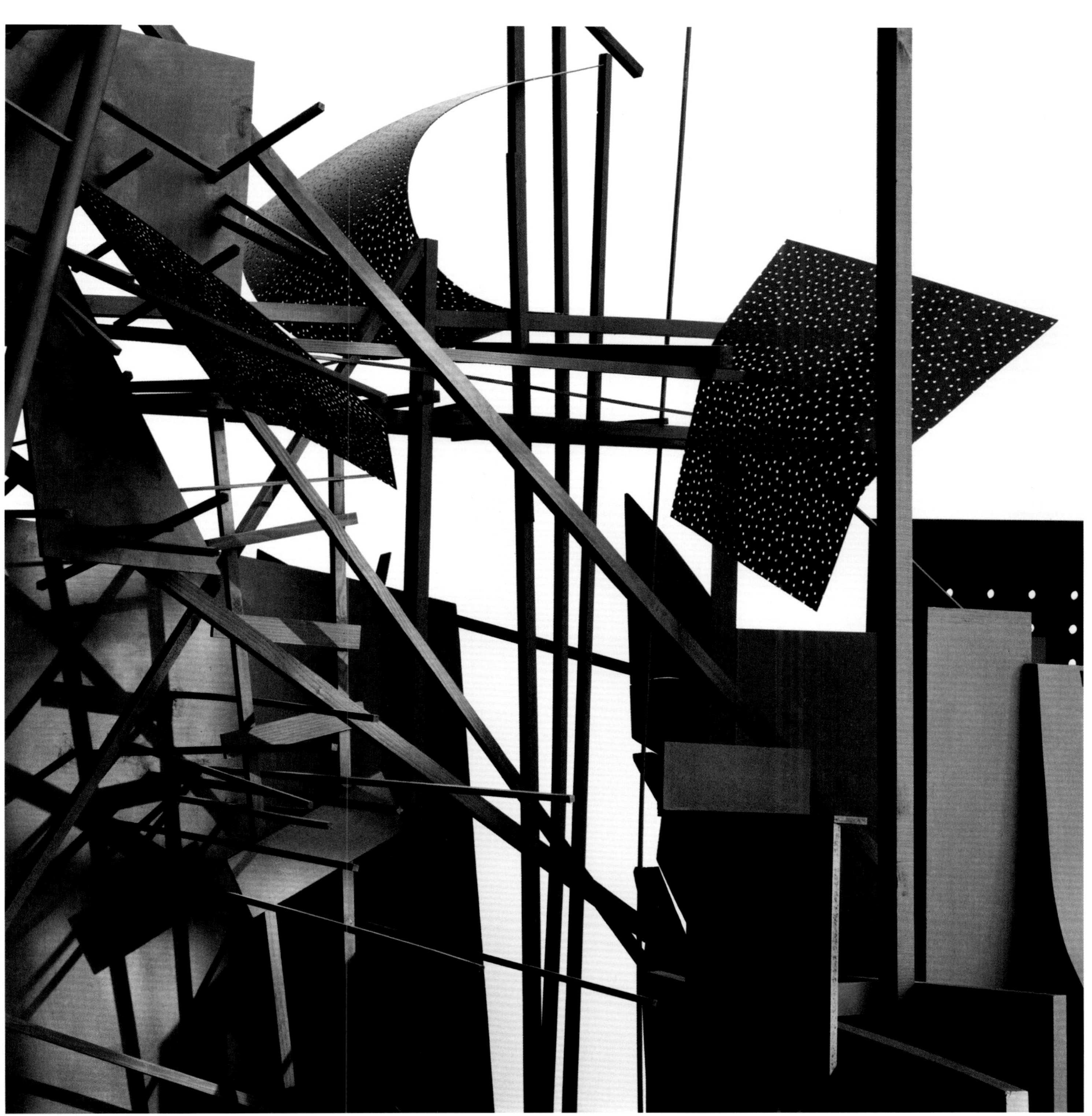

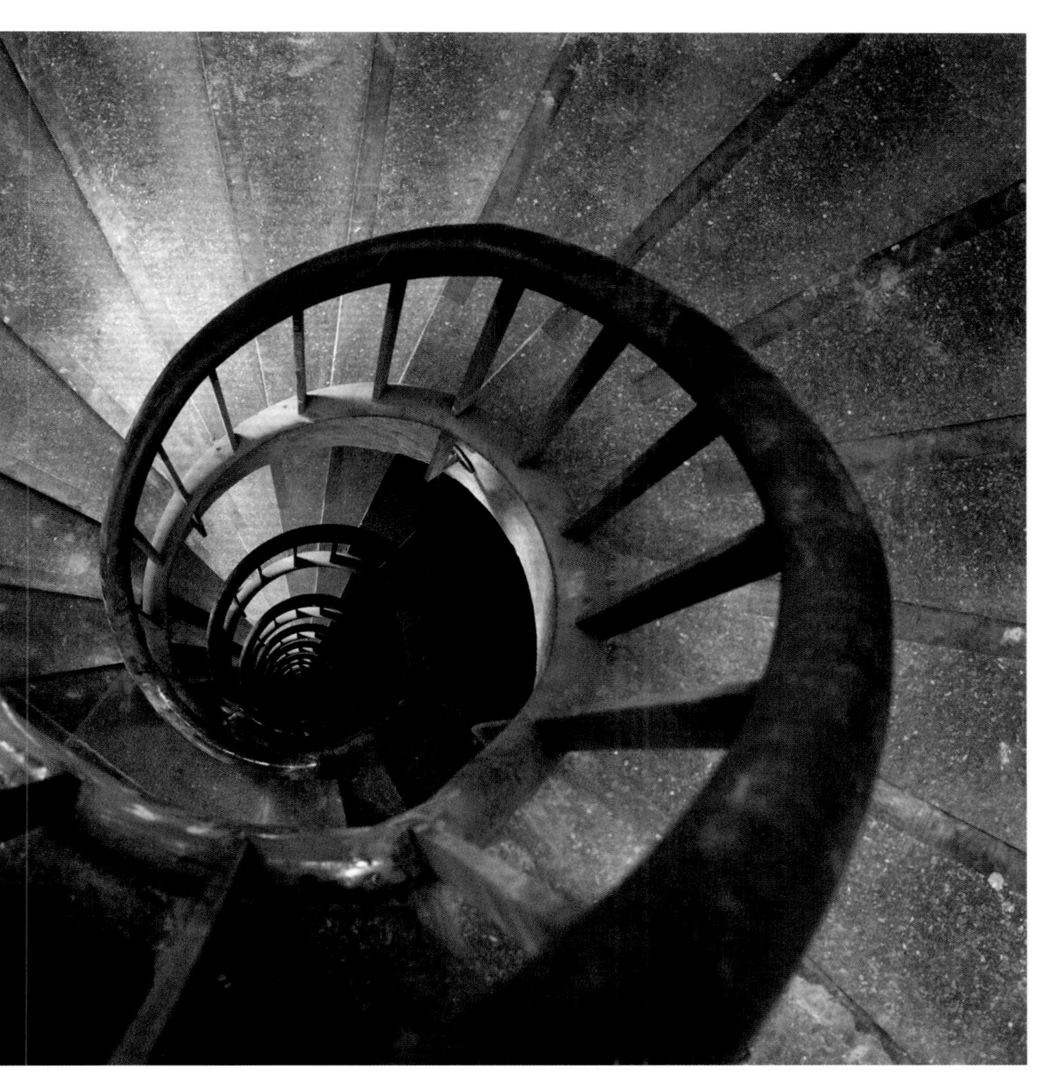

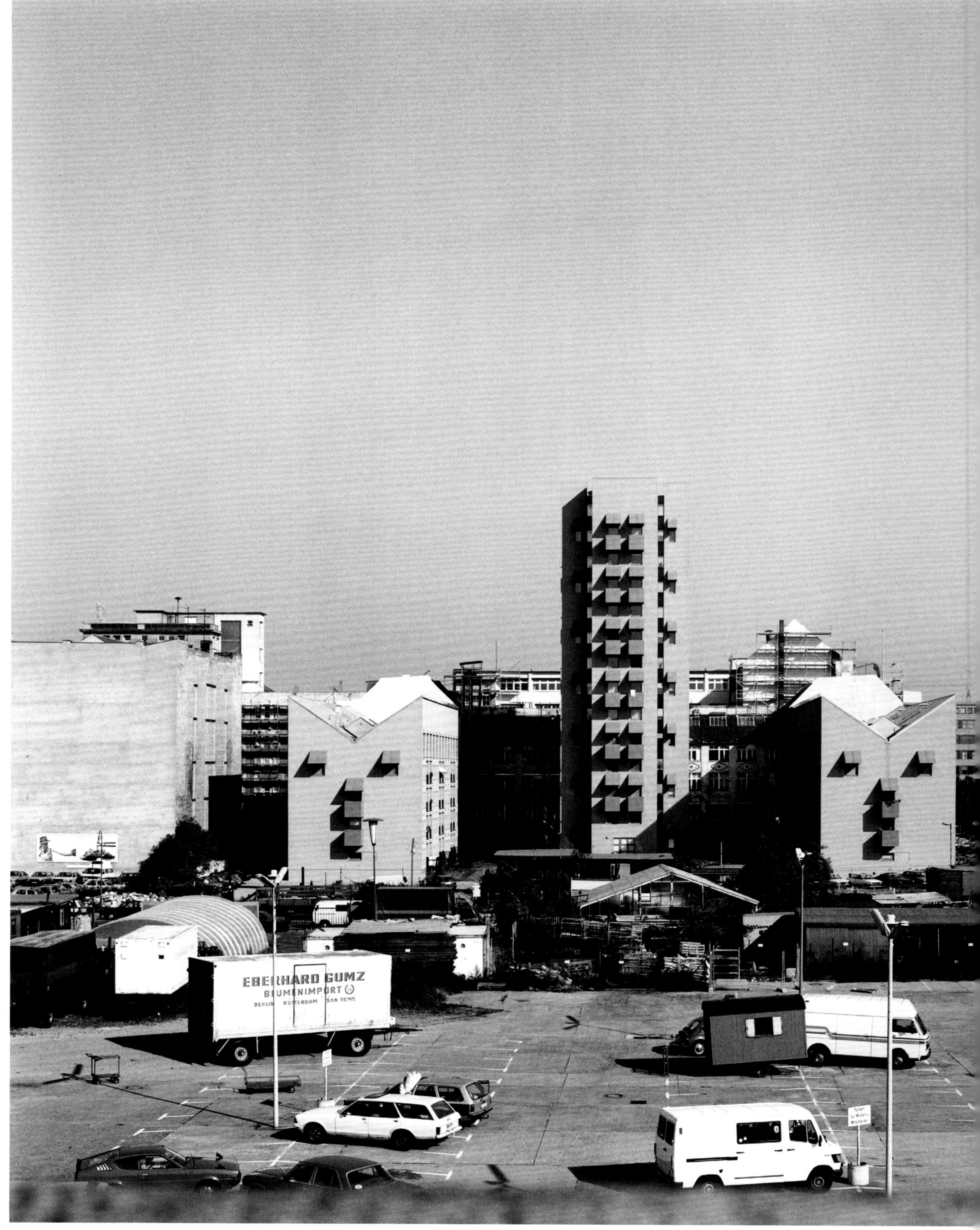

EBERHARD GUMZ
BLUMENIMPORT
BERLIN · ROTTERDAM · SAN REMO

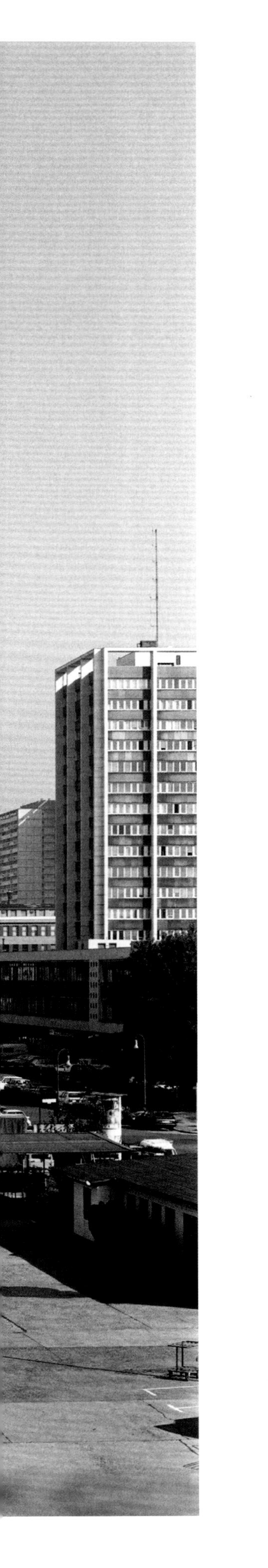

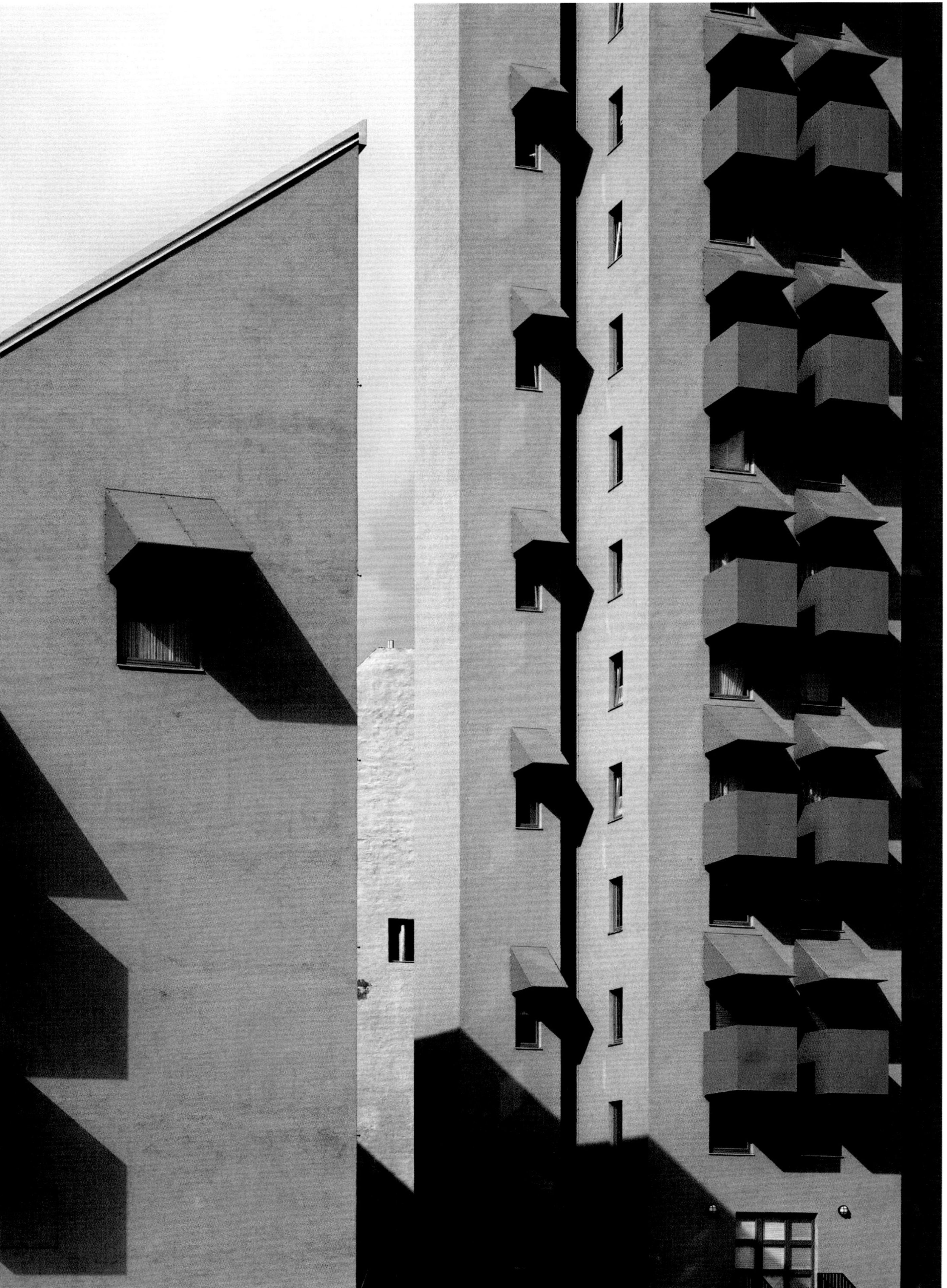

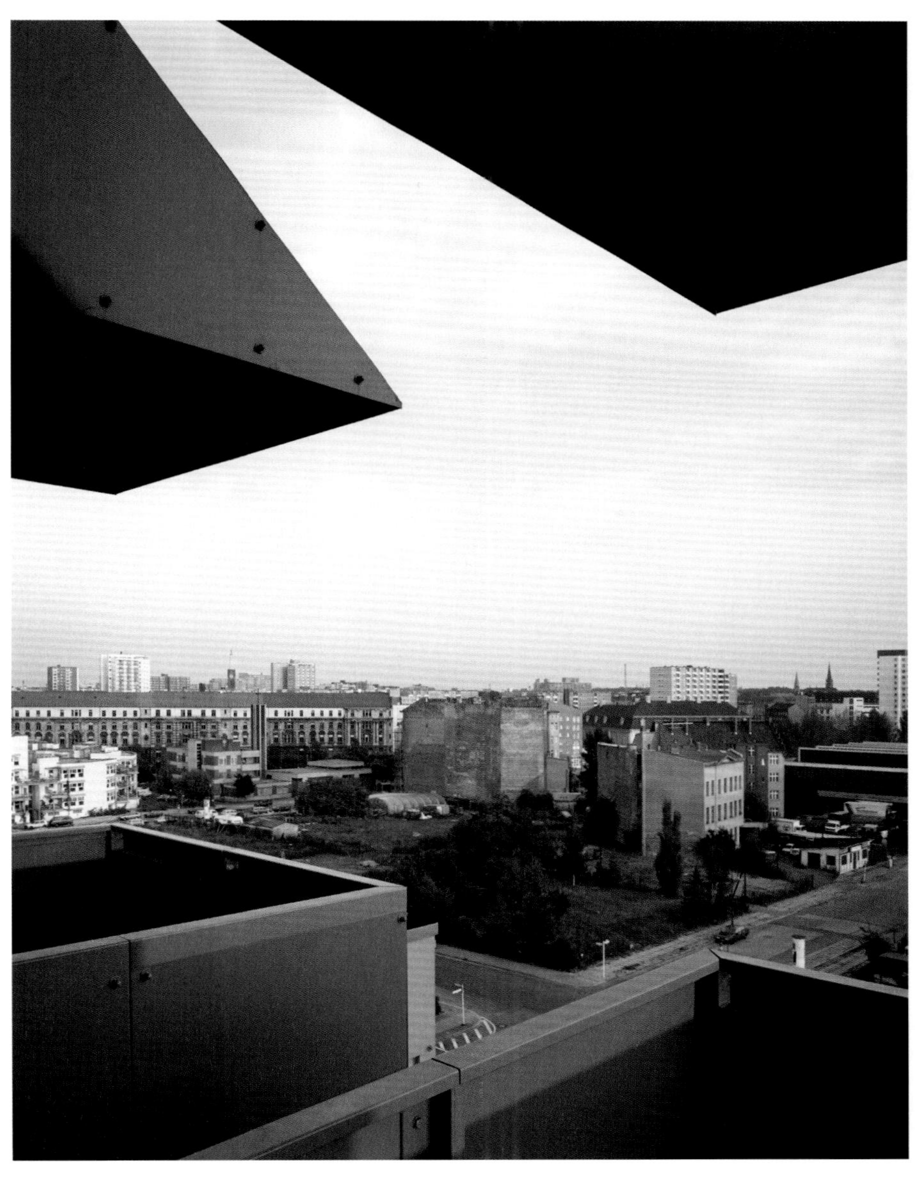

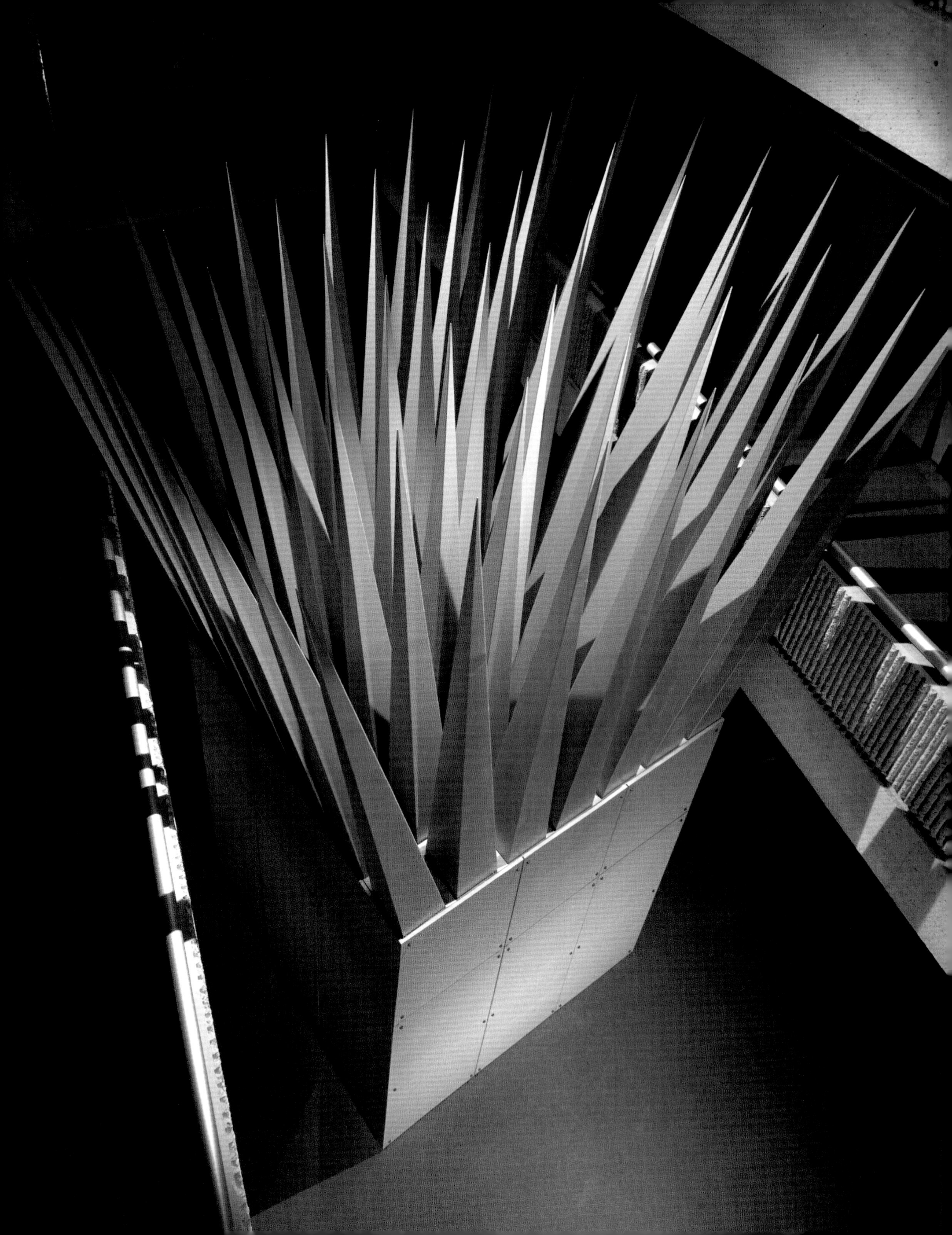

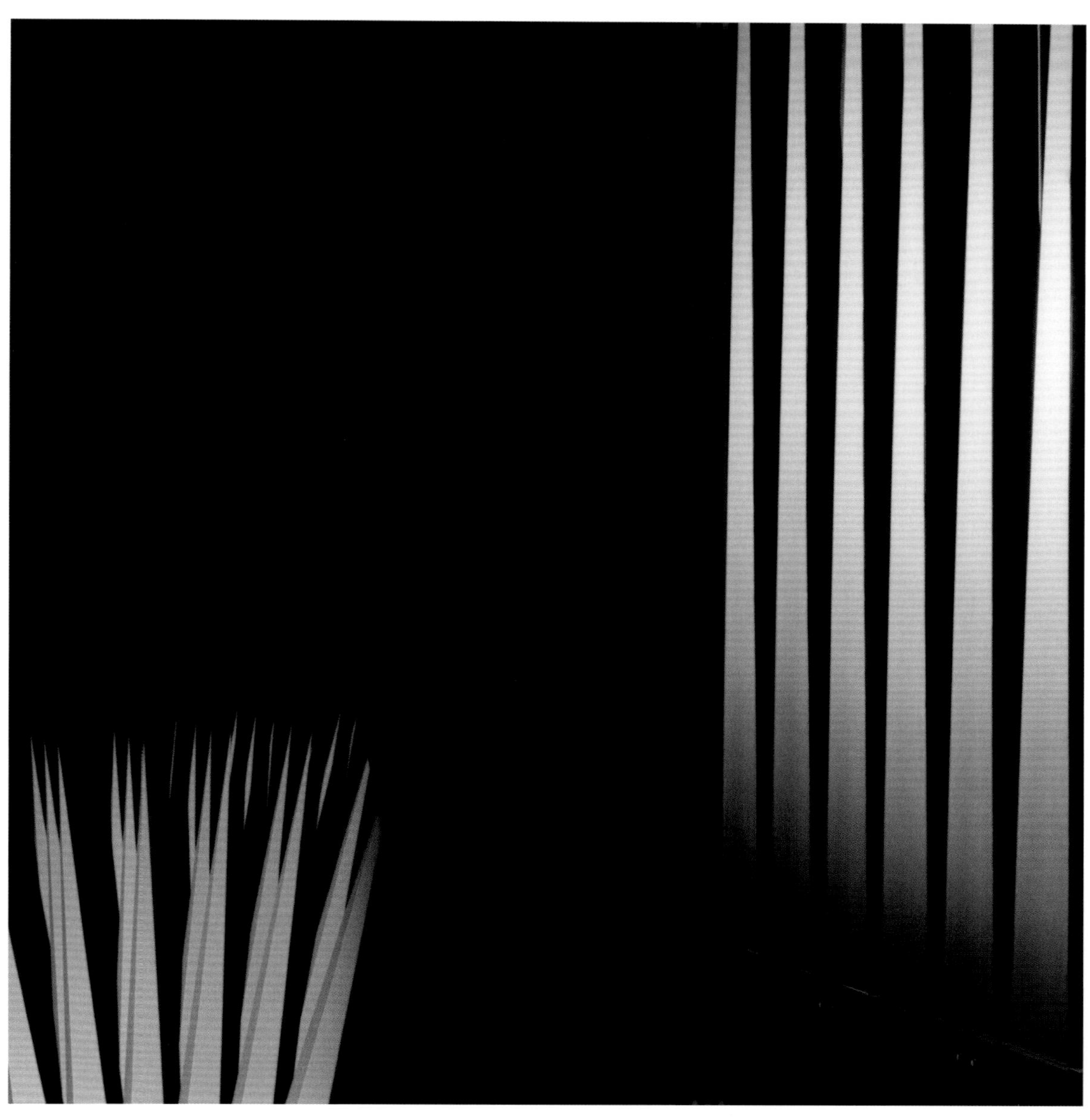

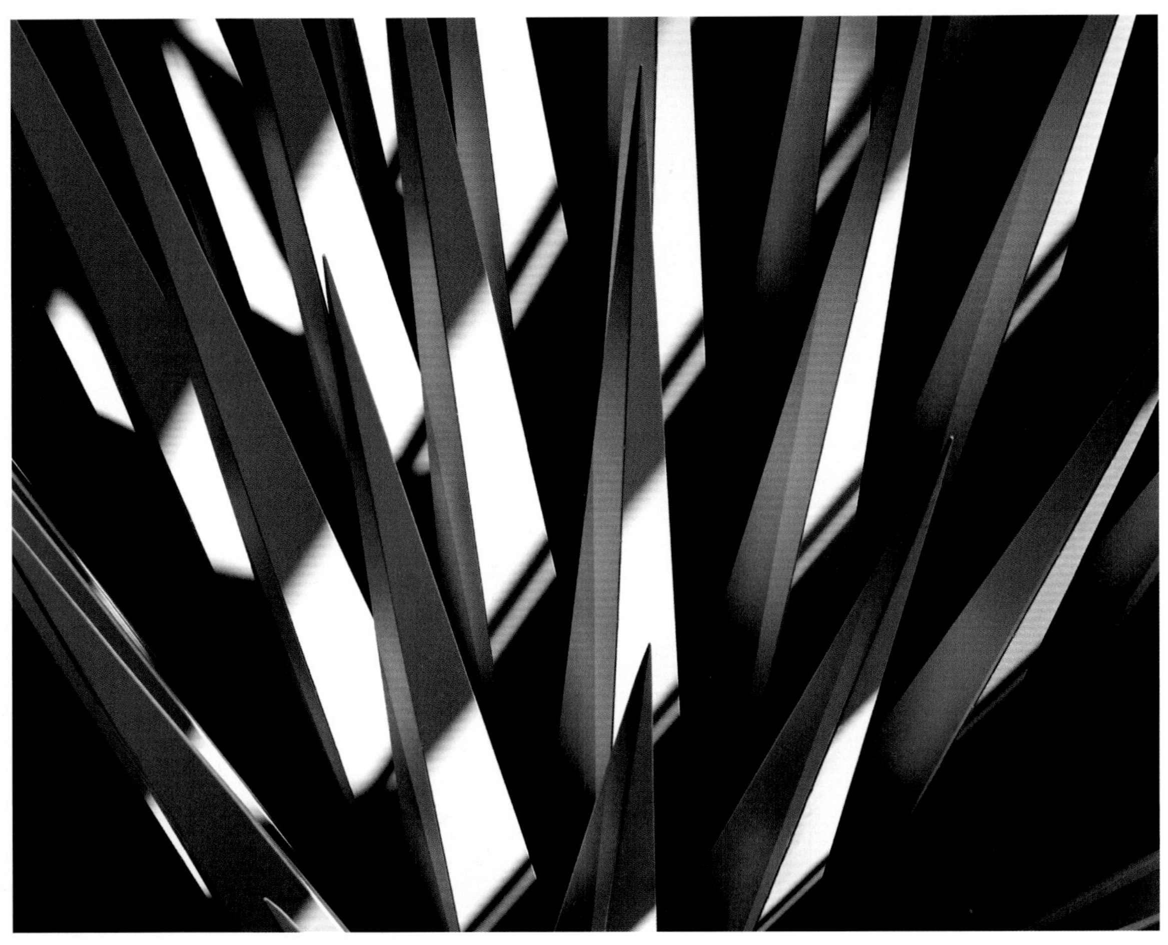

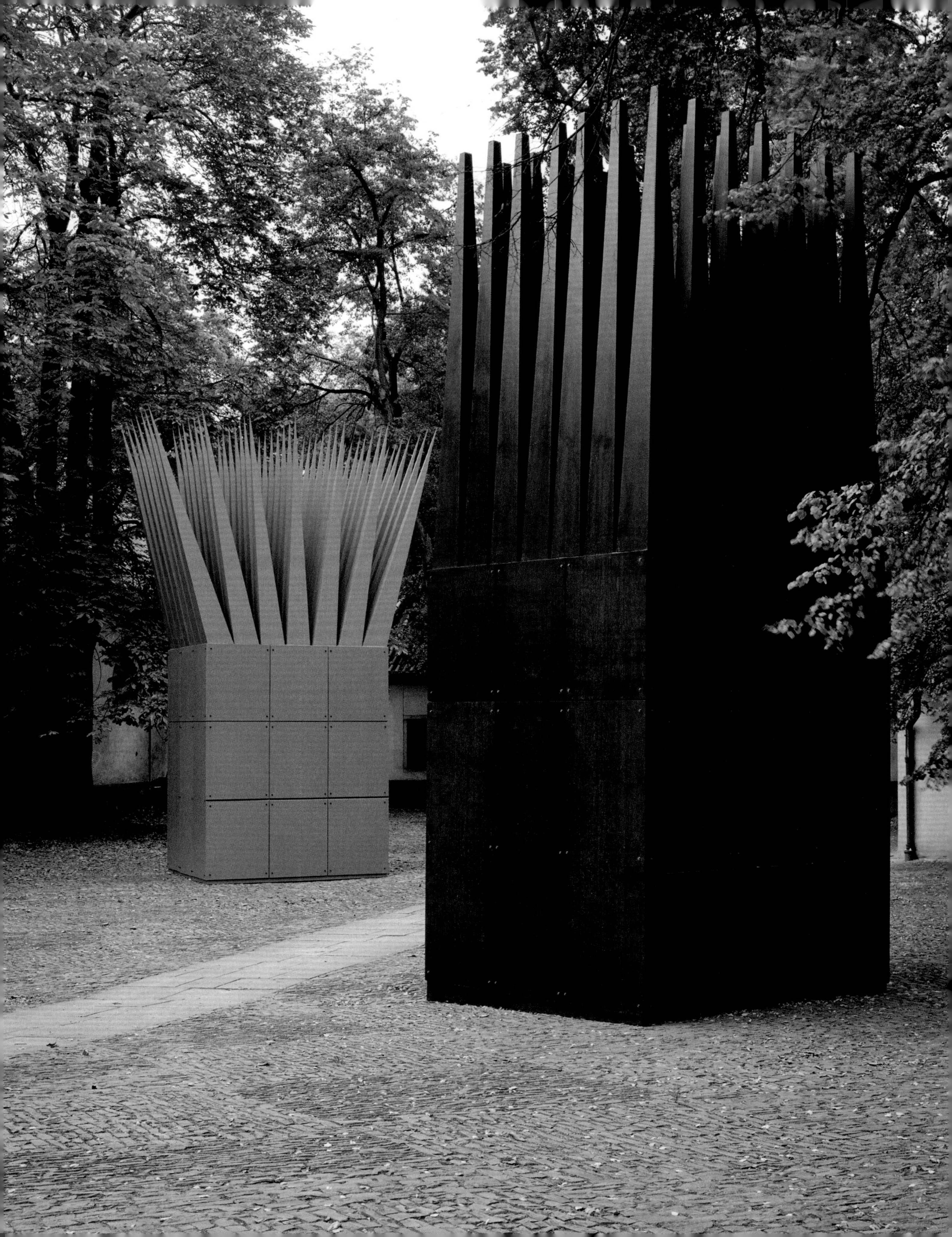

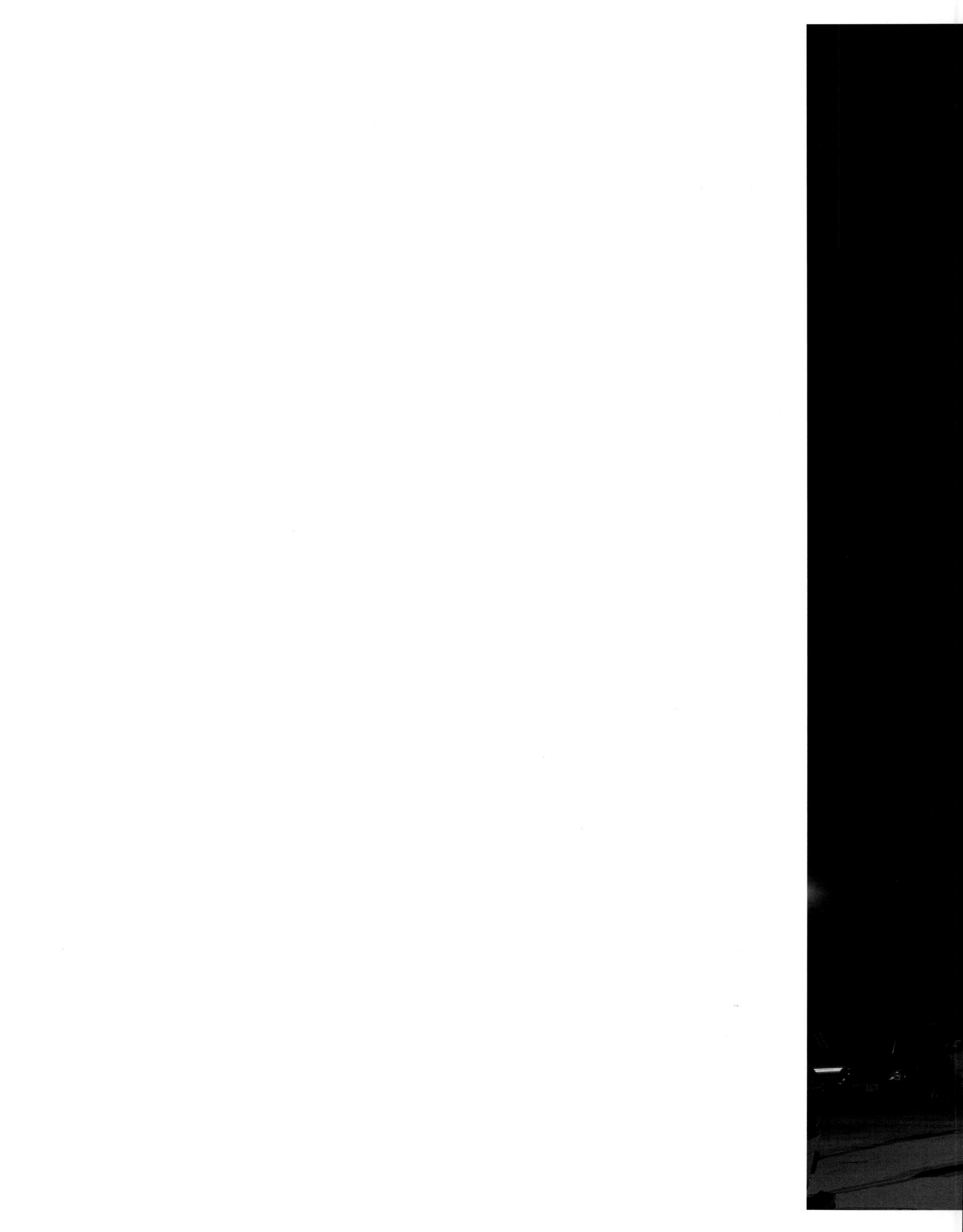

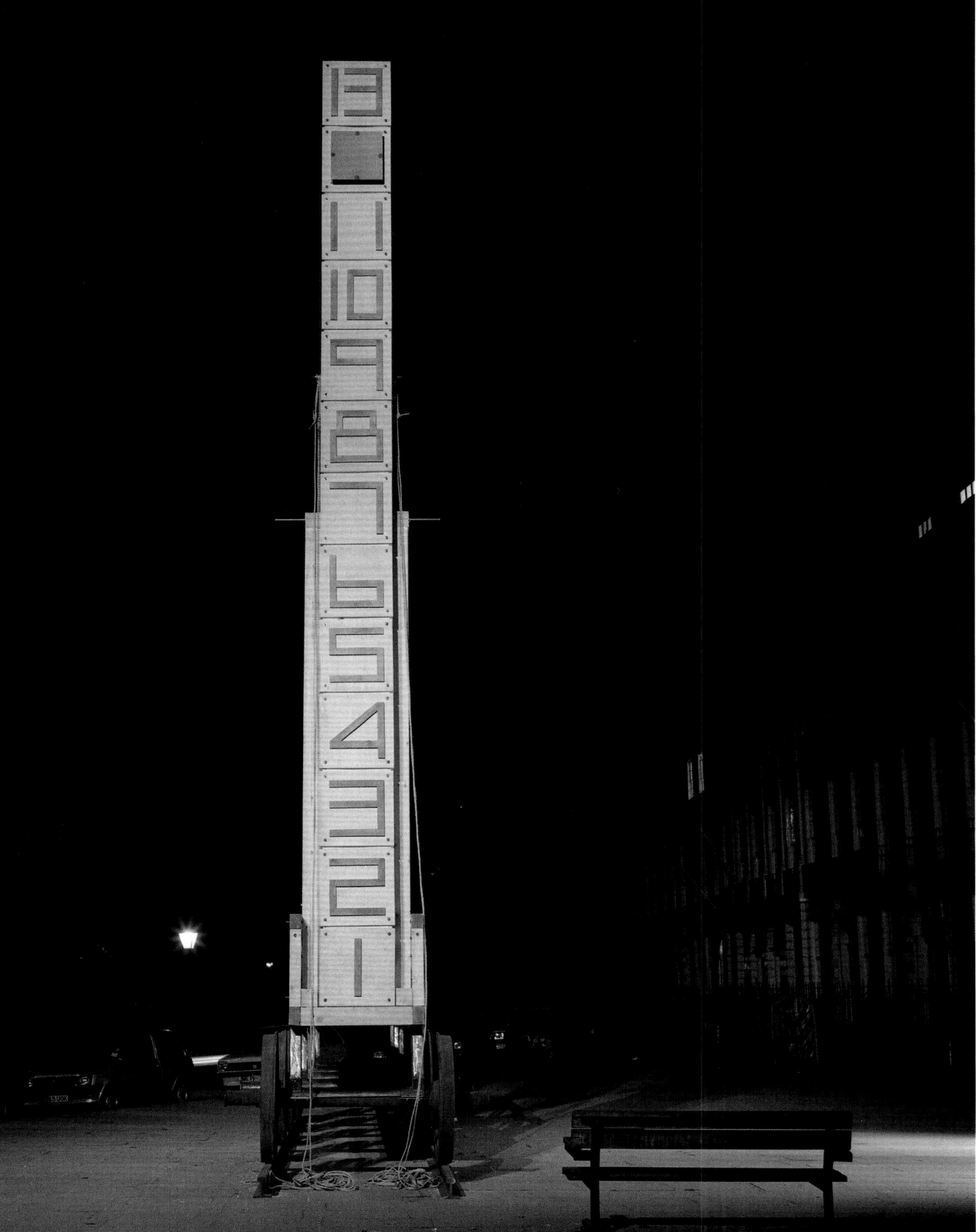

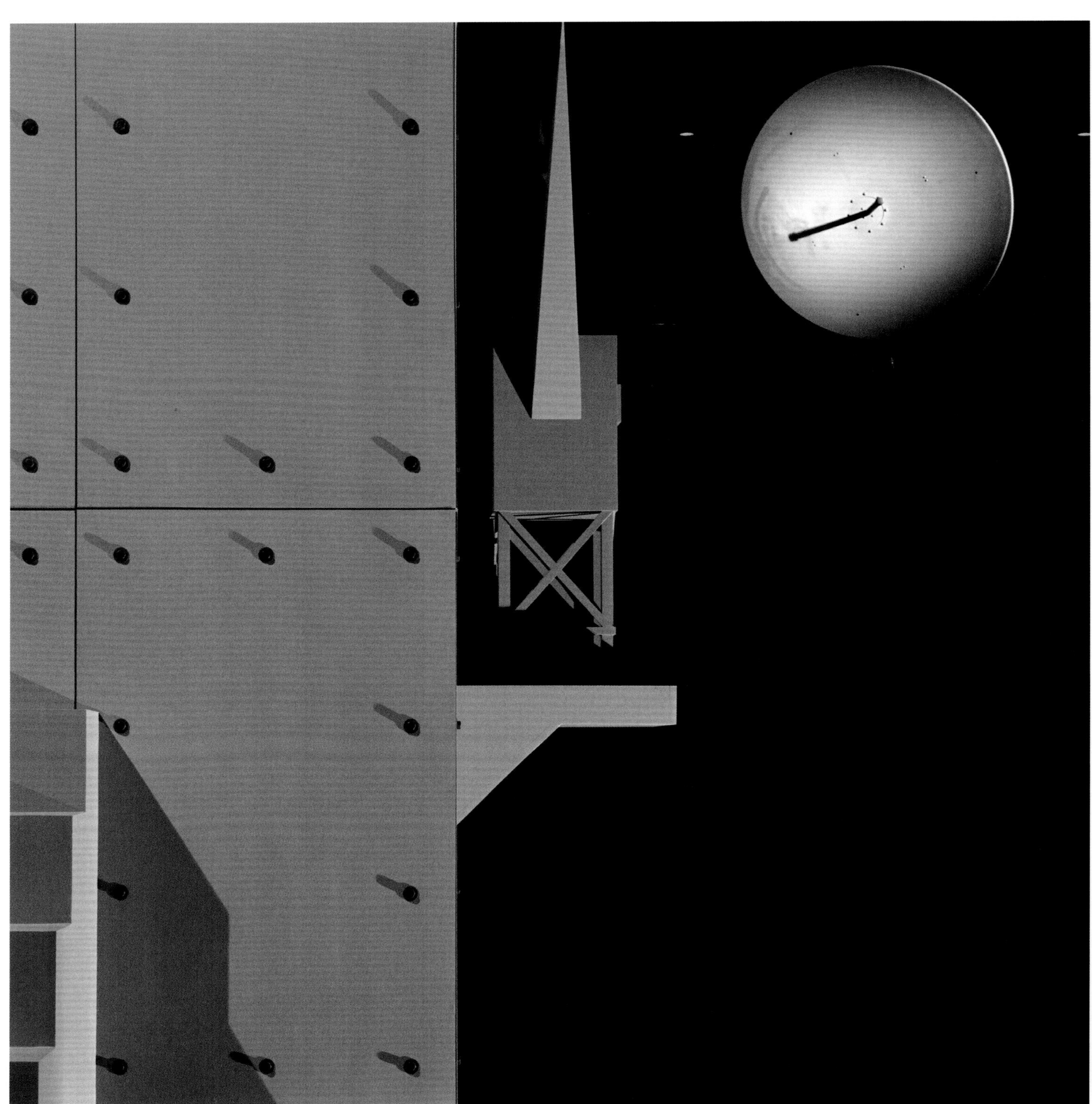

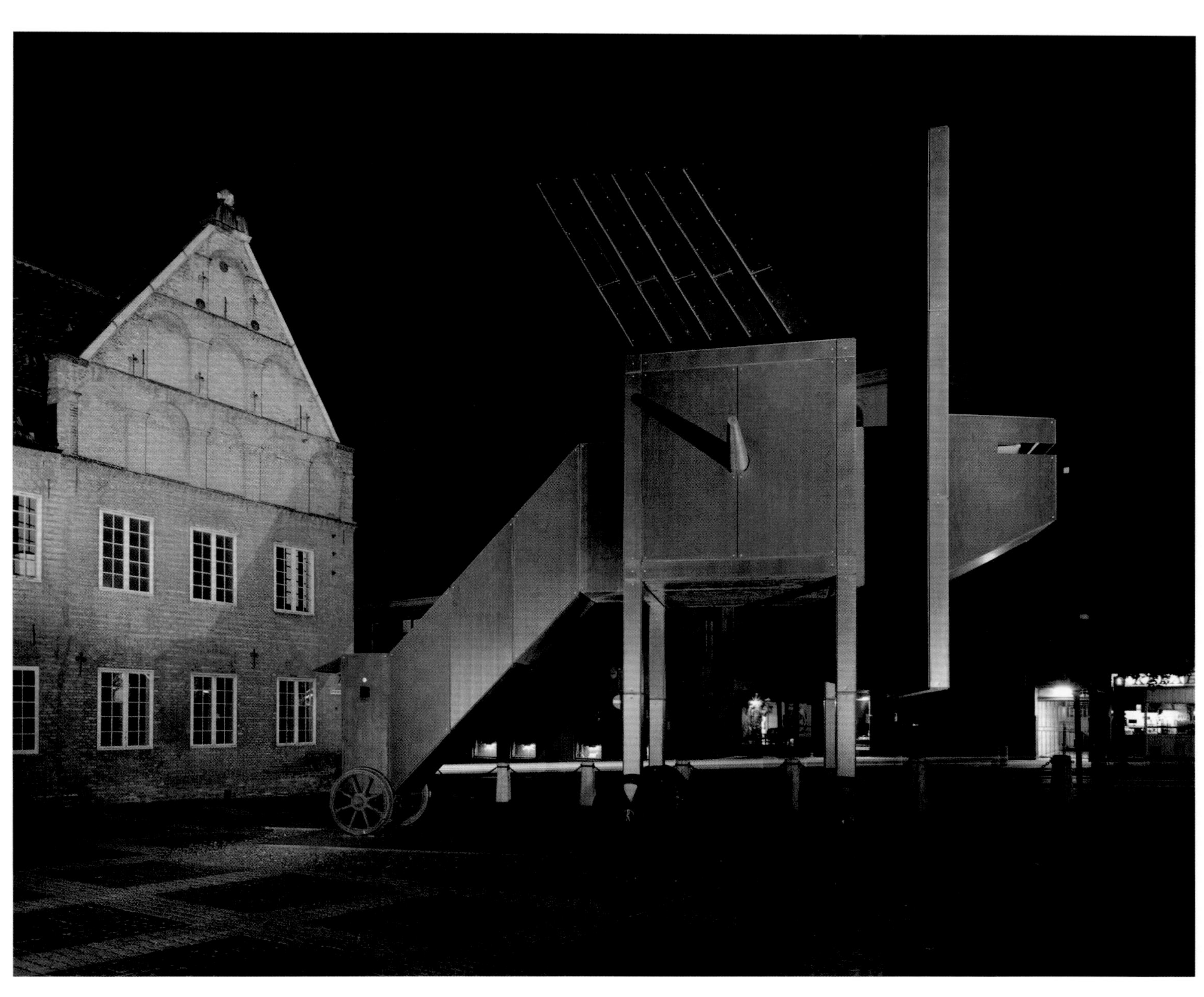

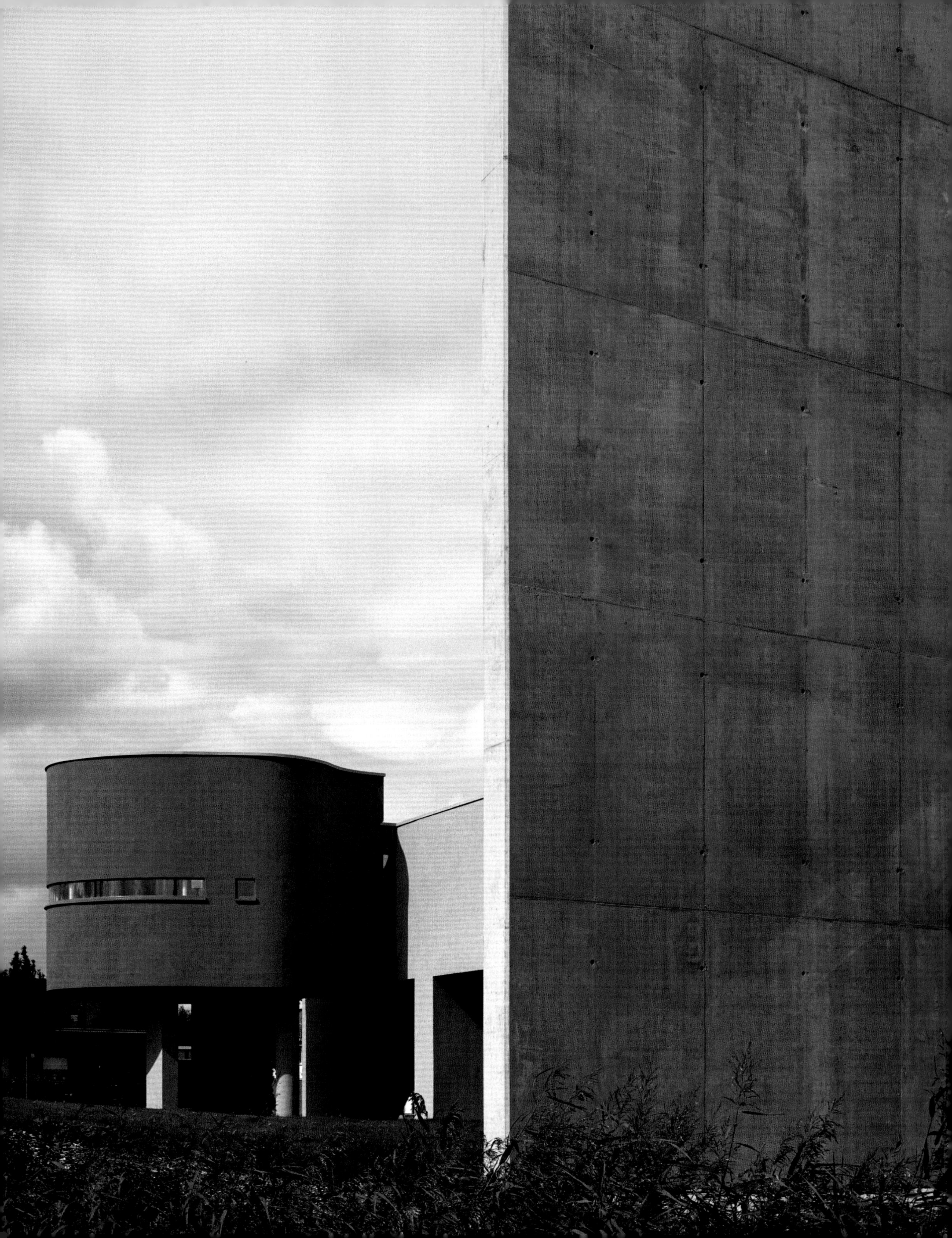

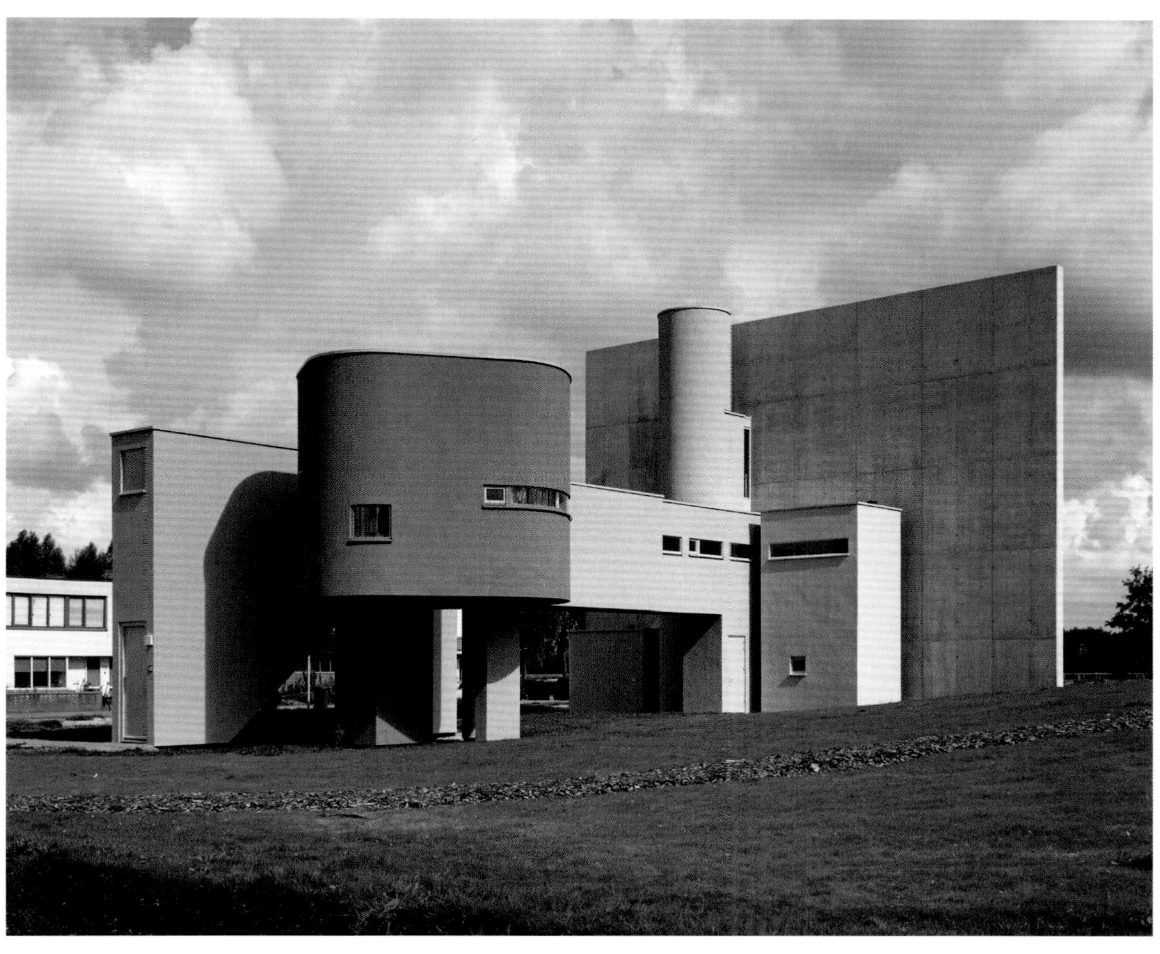

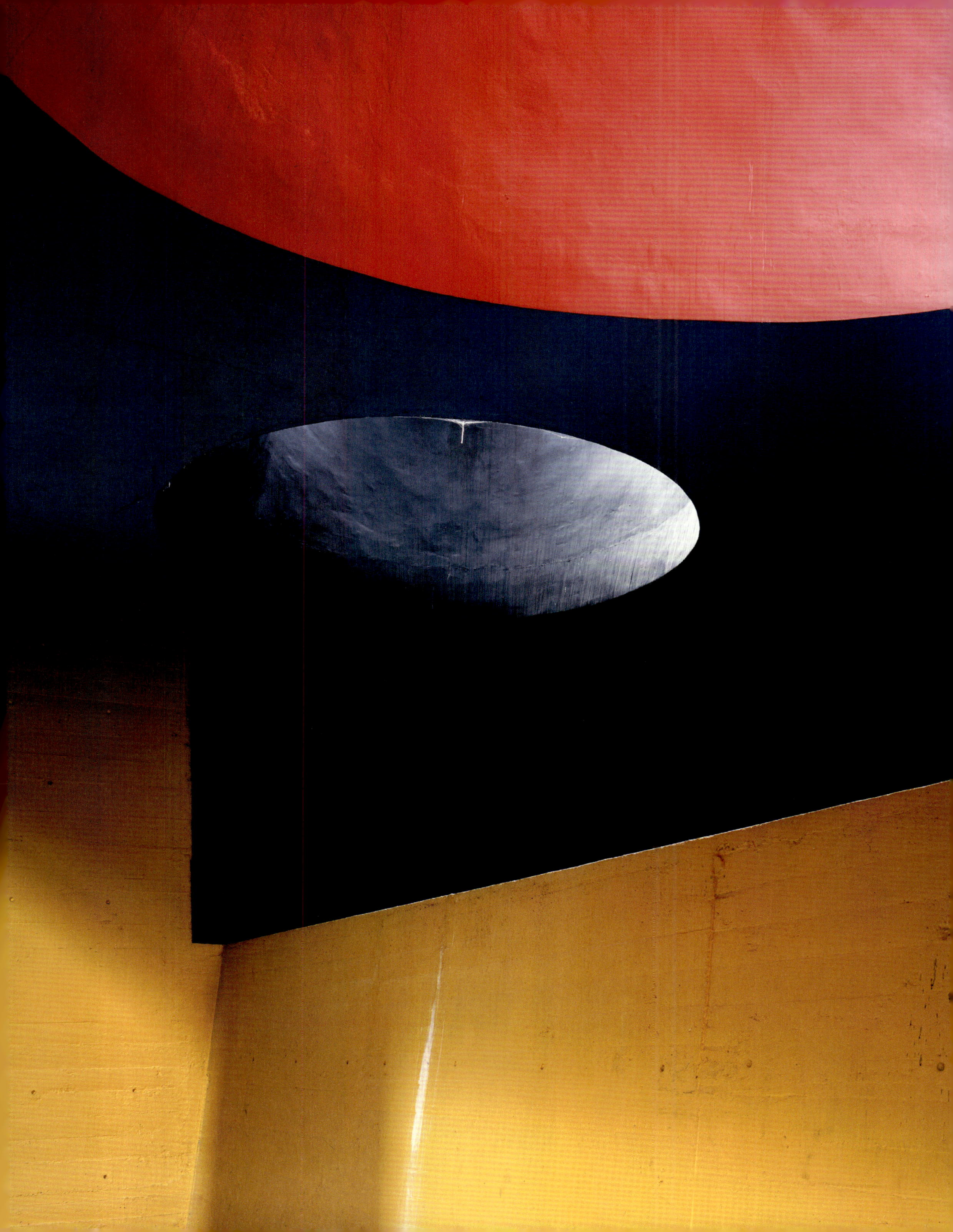

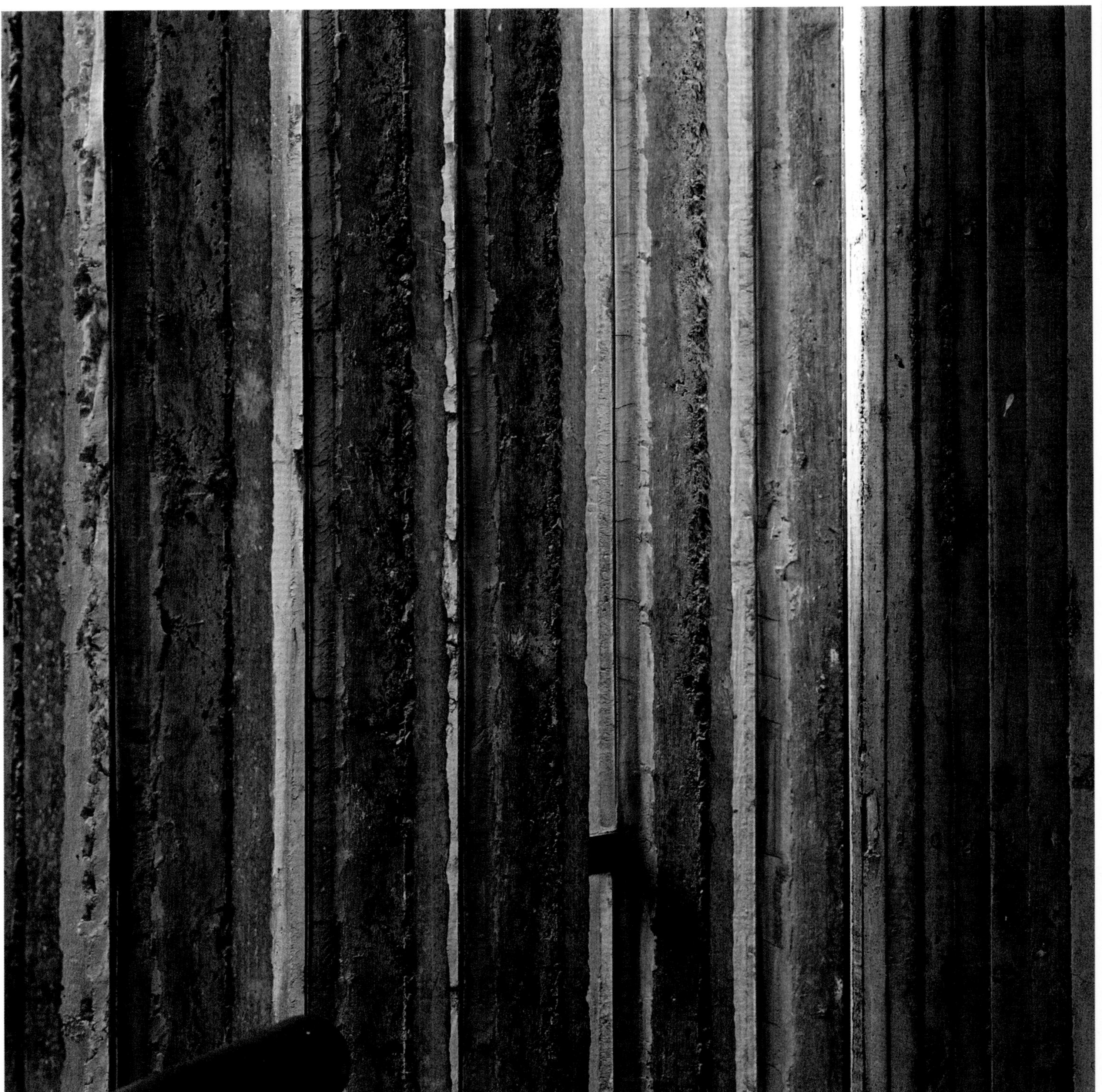

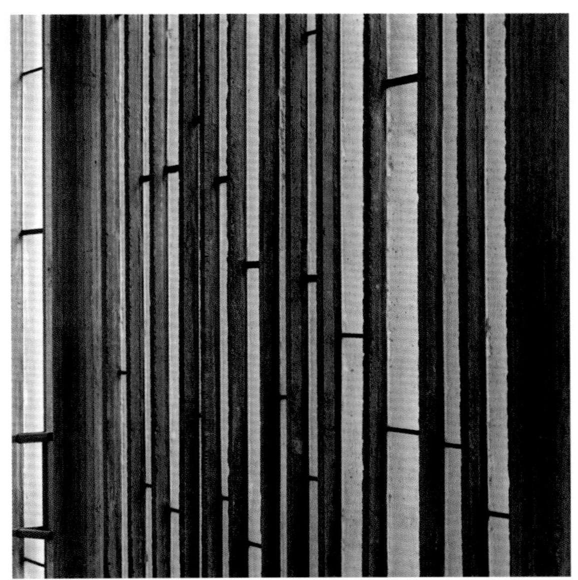

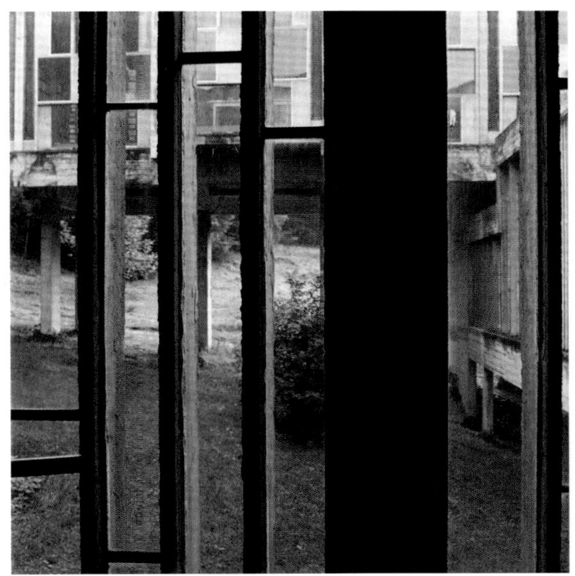

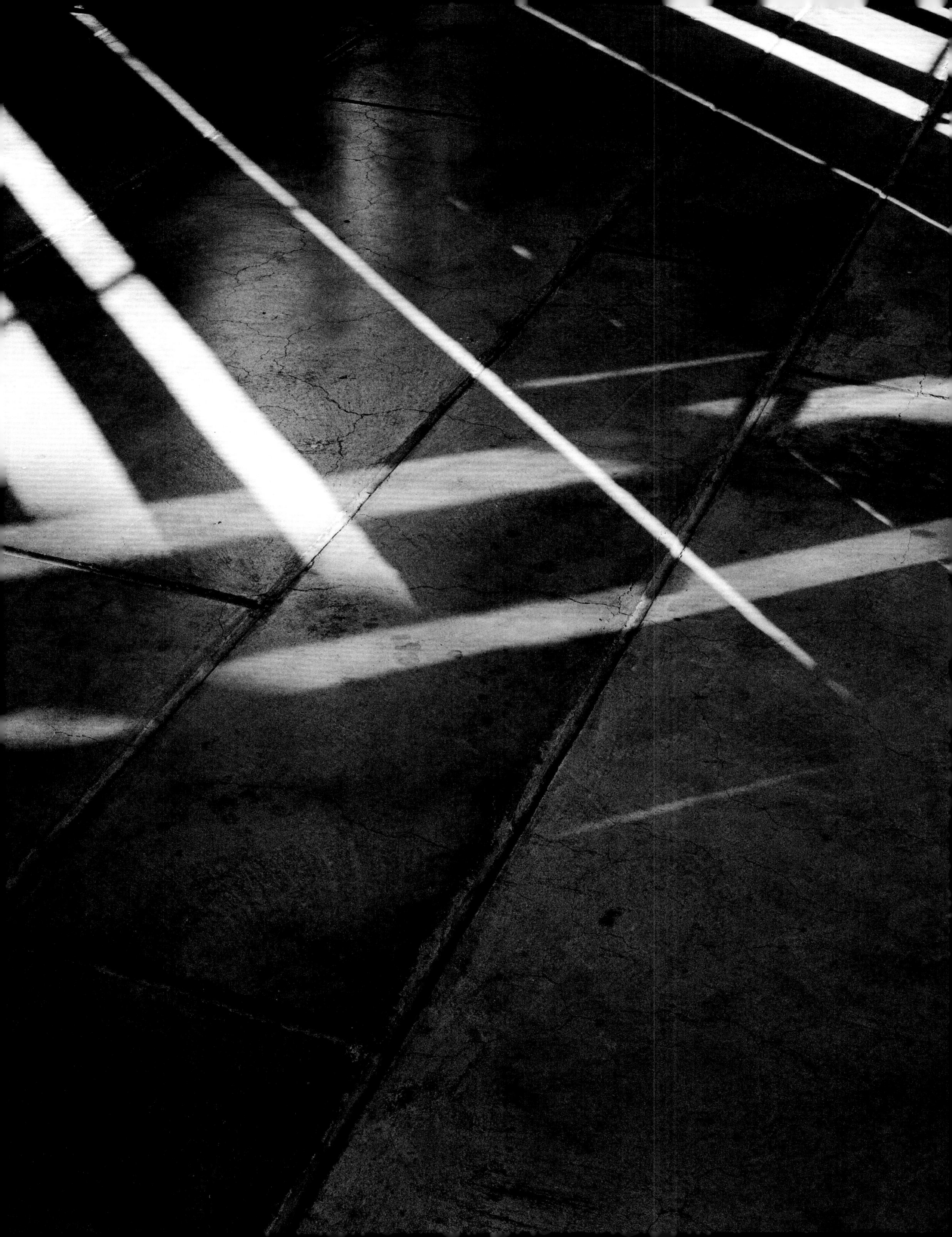

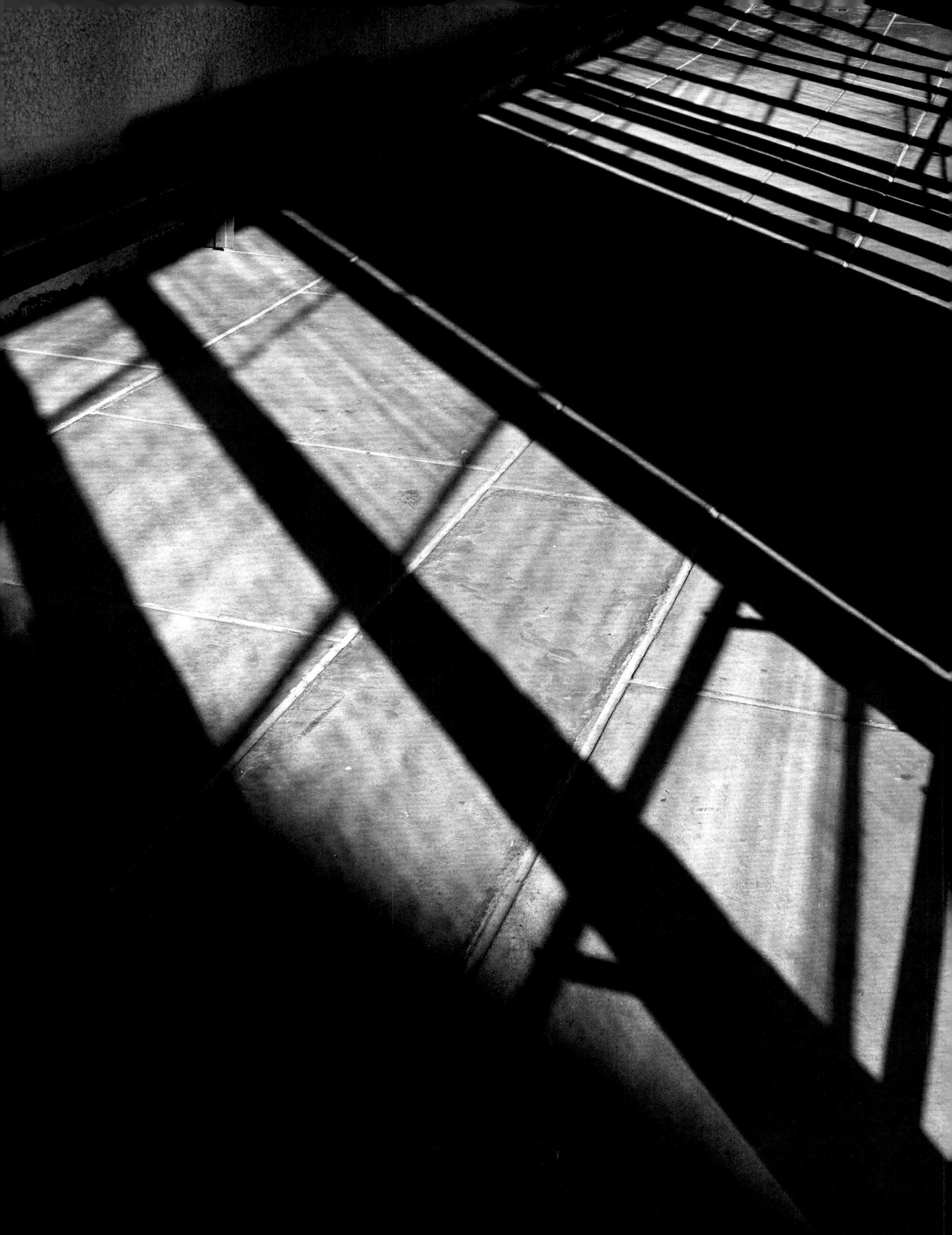

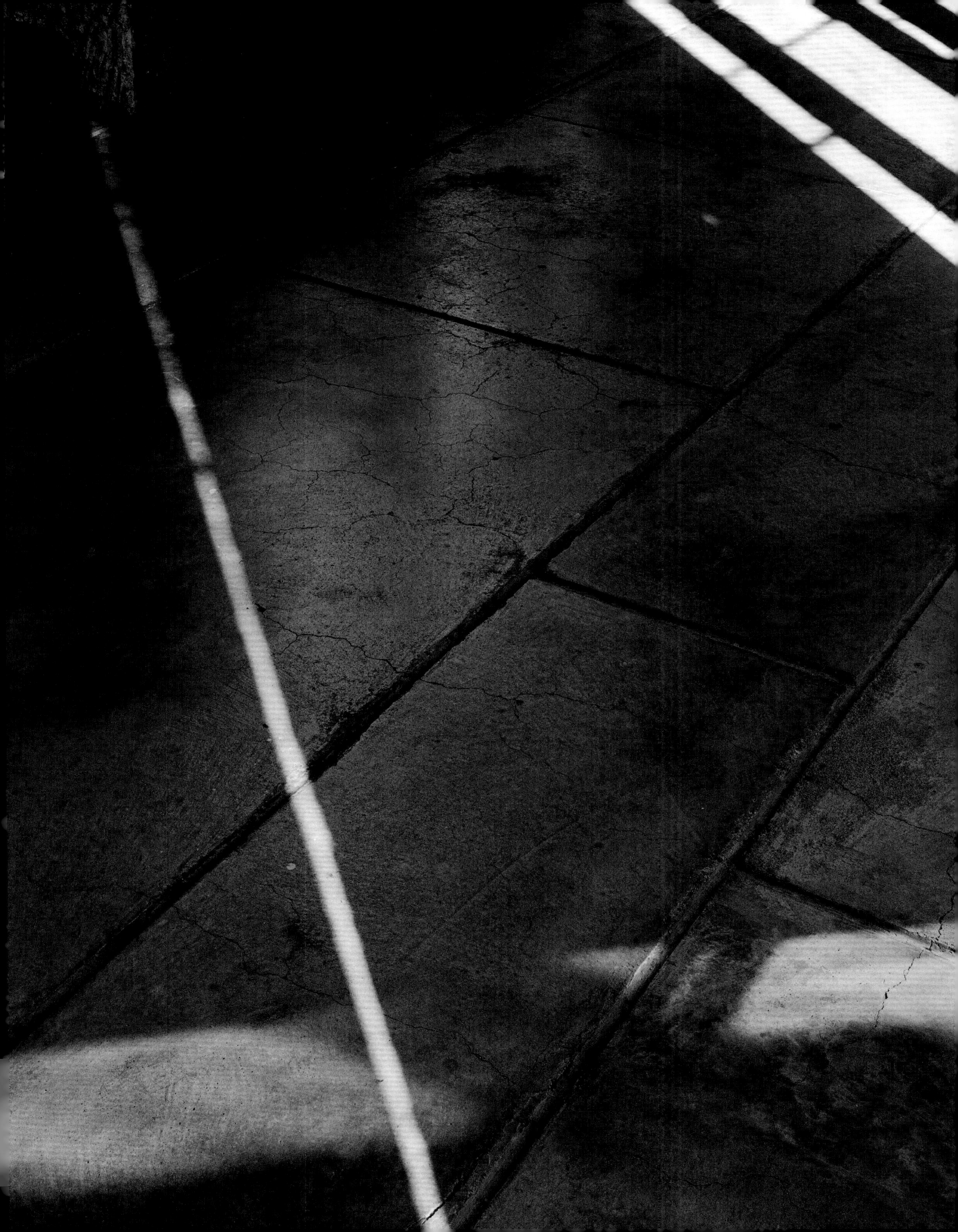

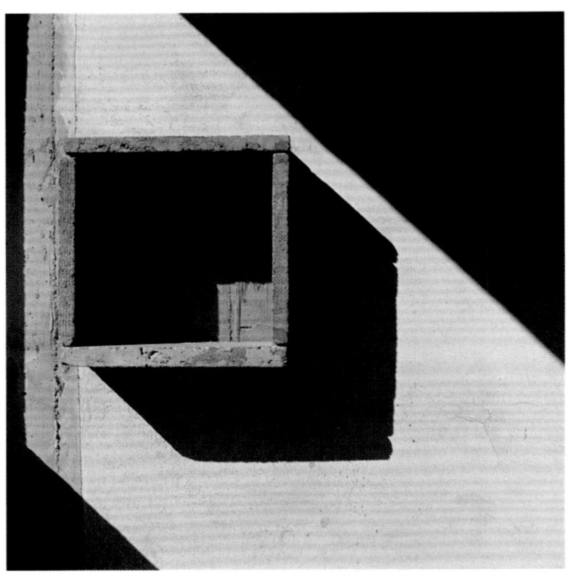
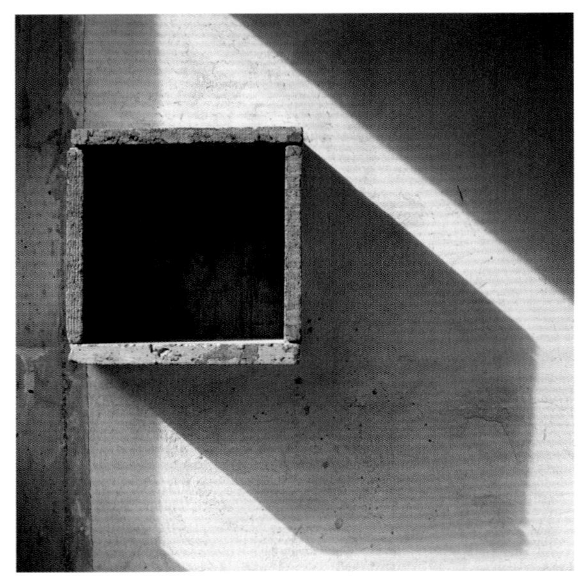

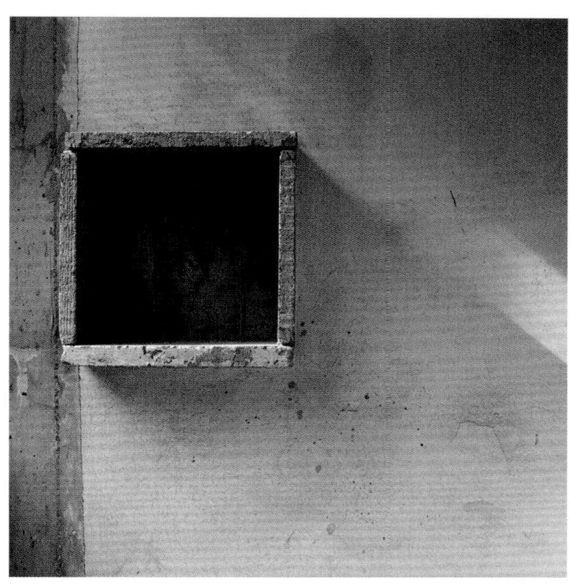 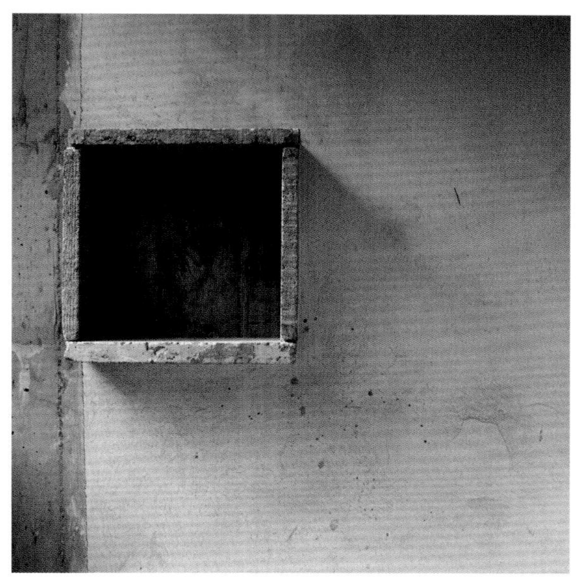

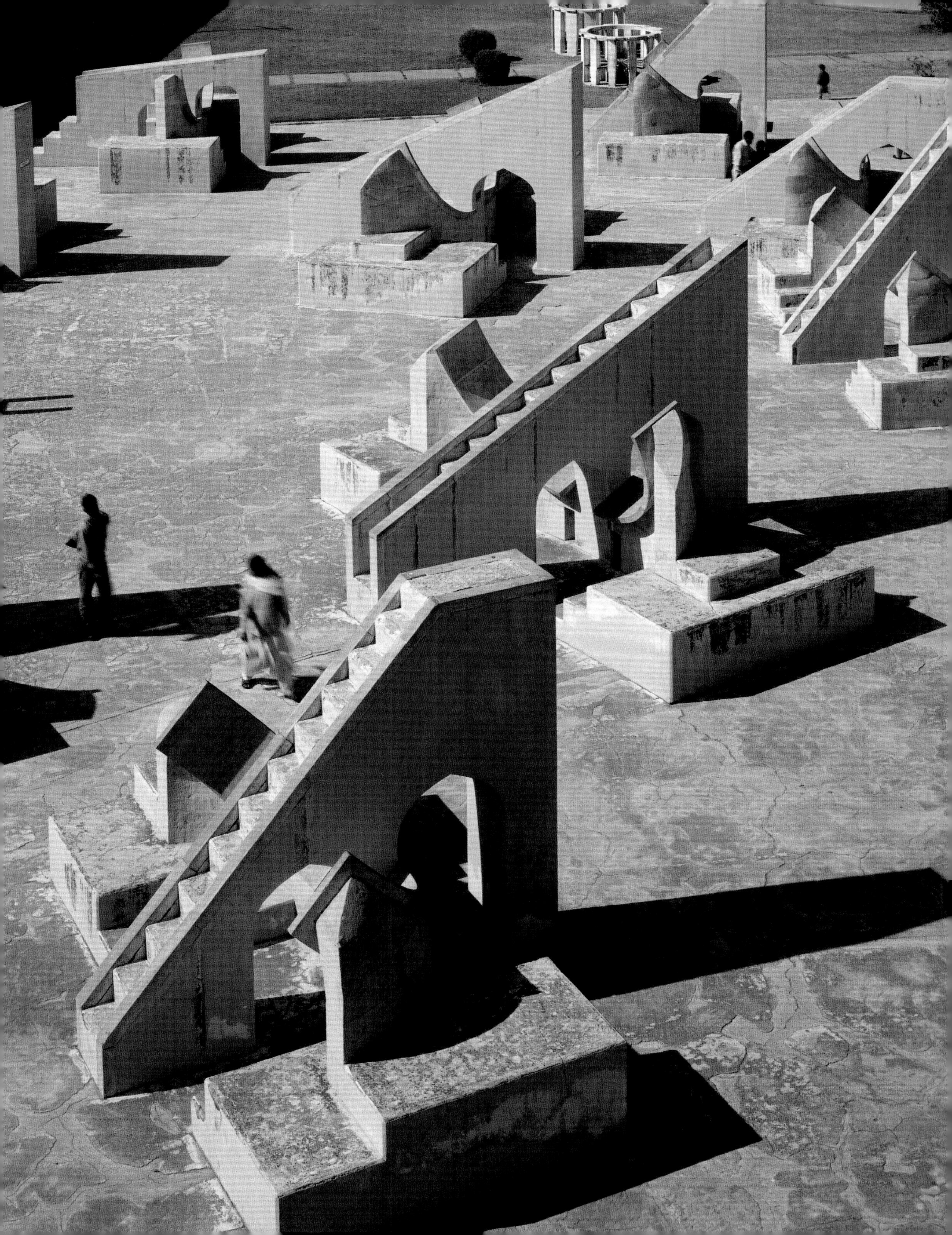

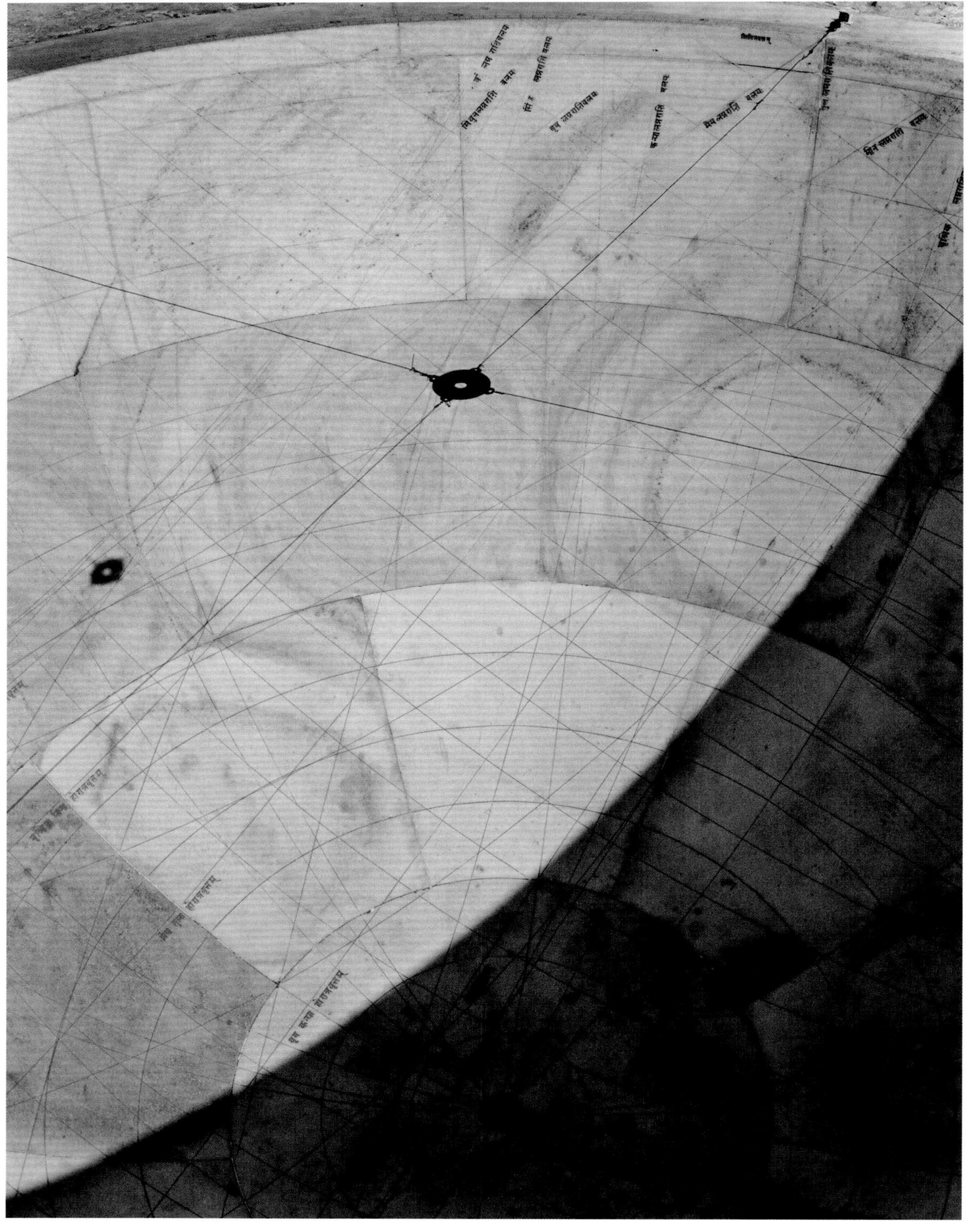

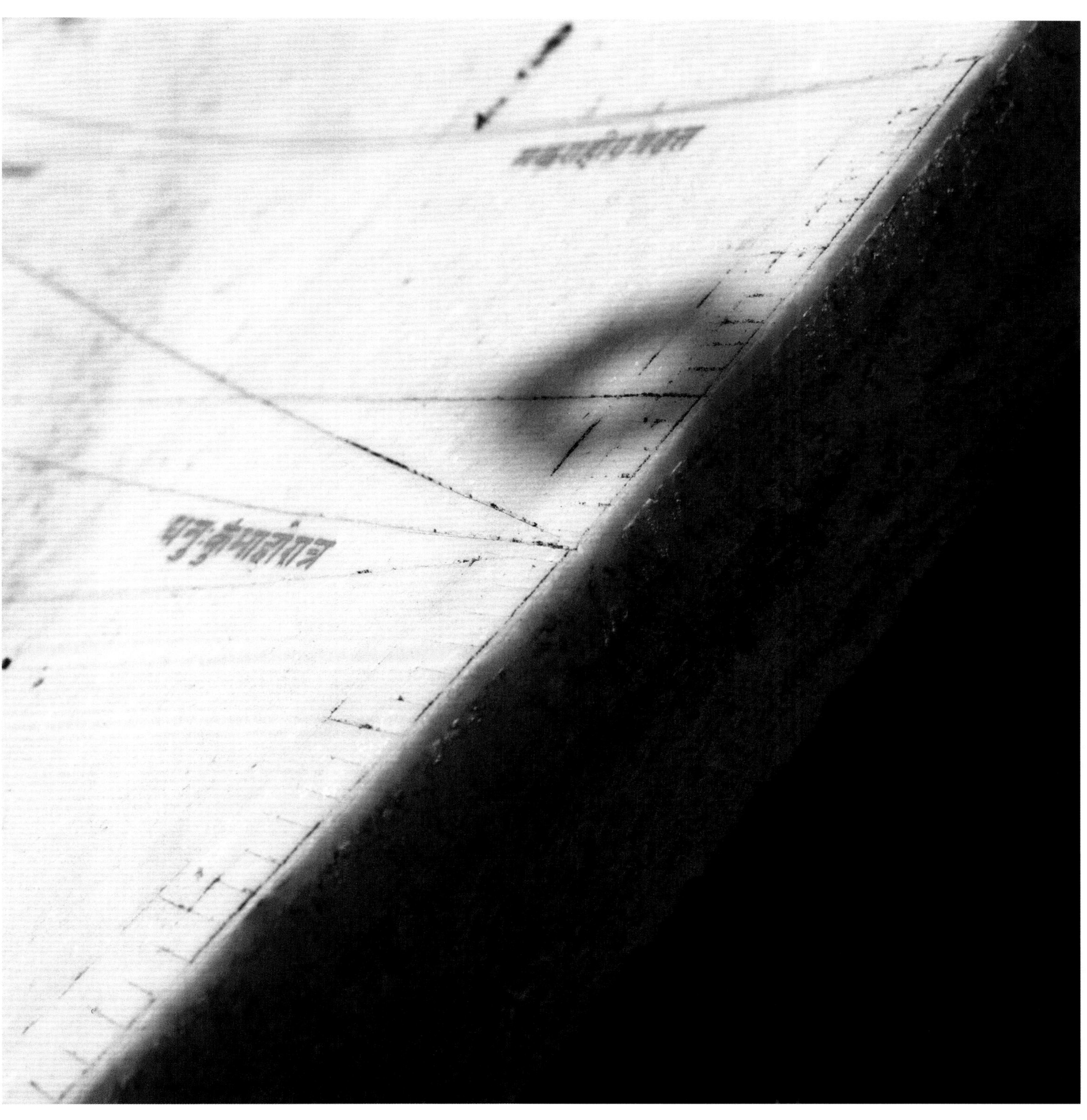

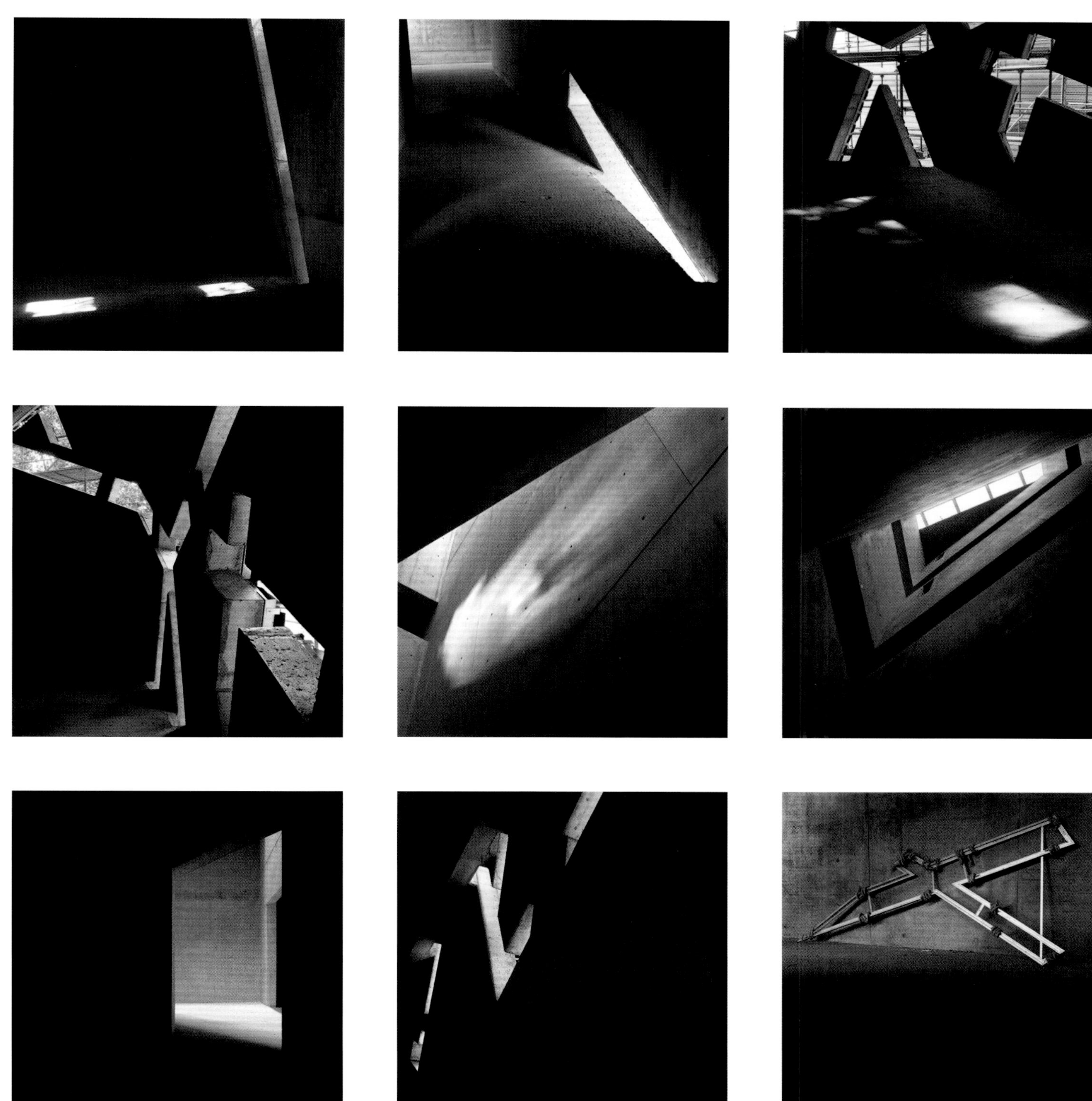

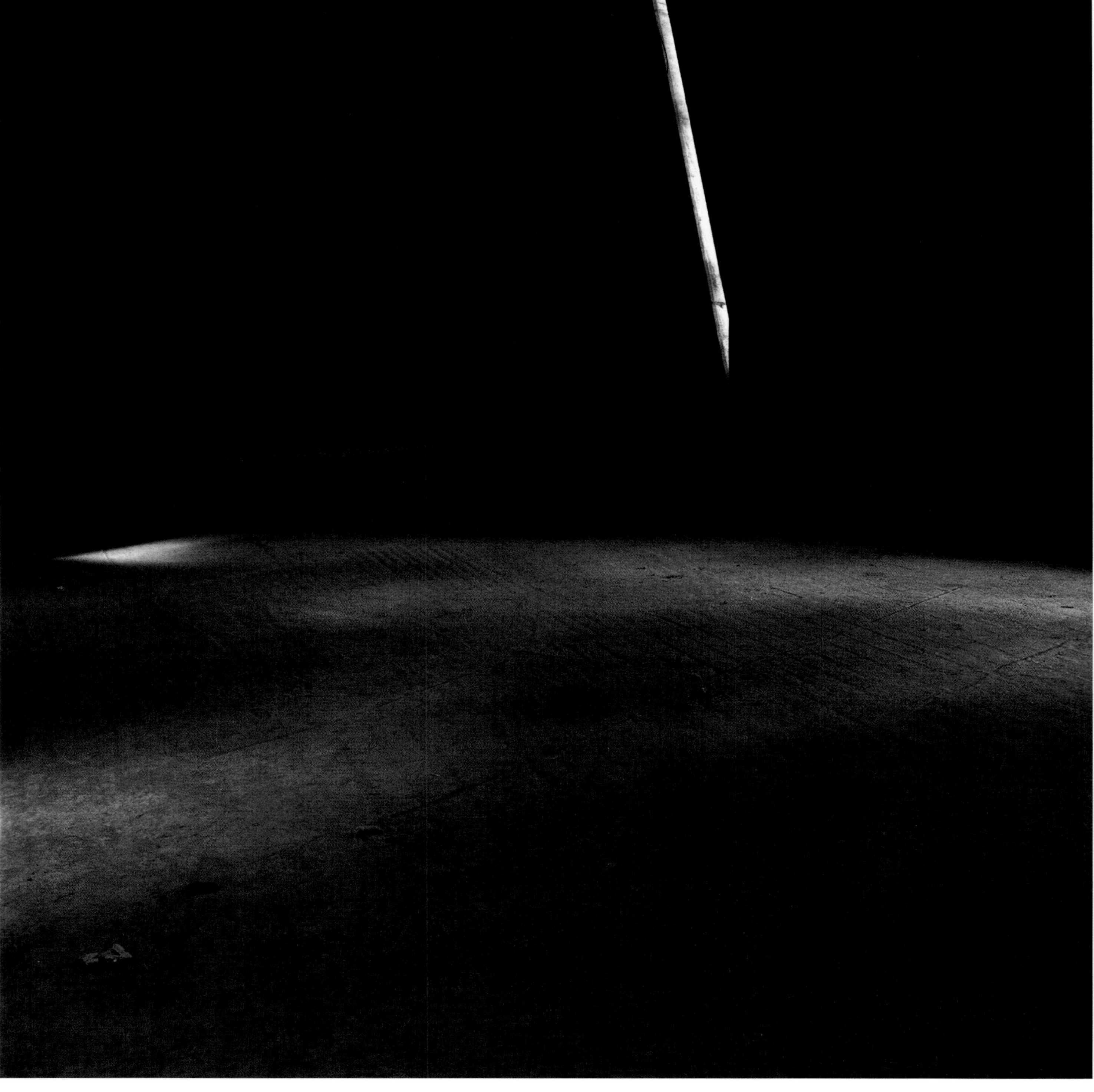

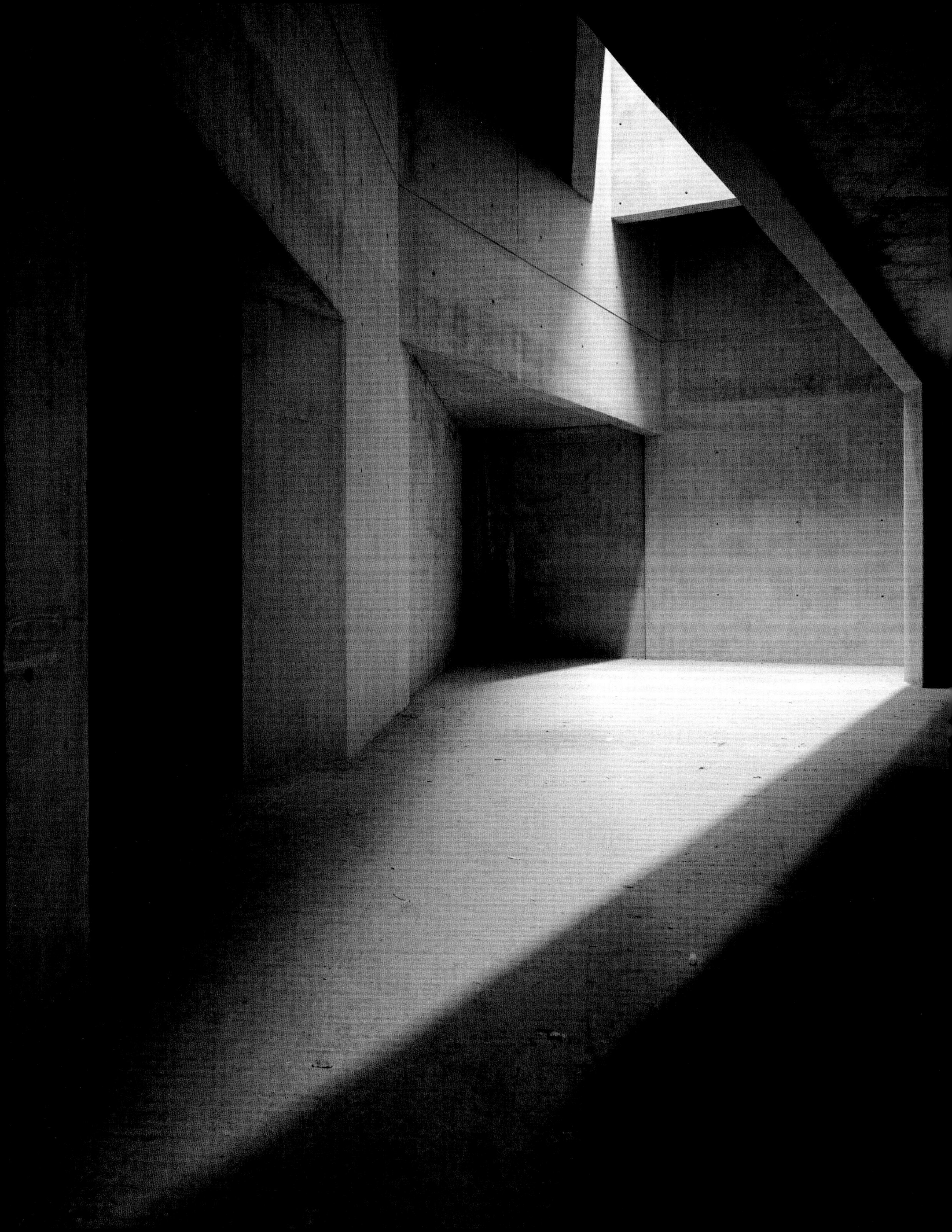

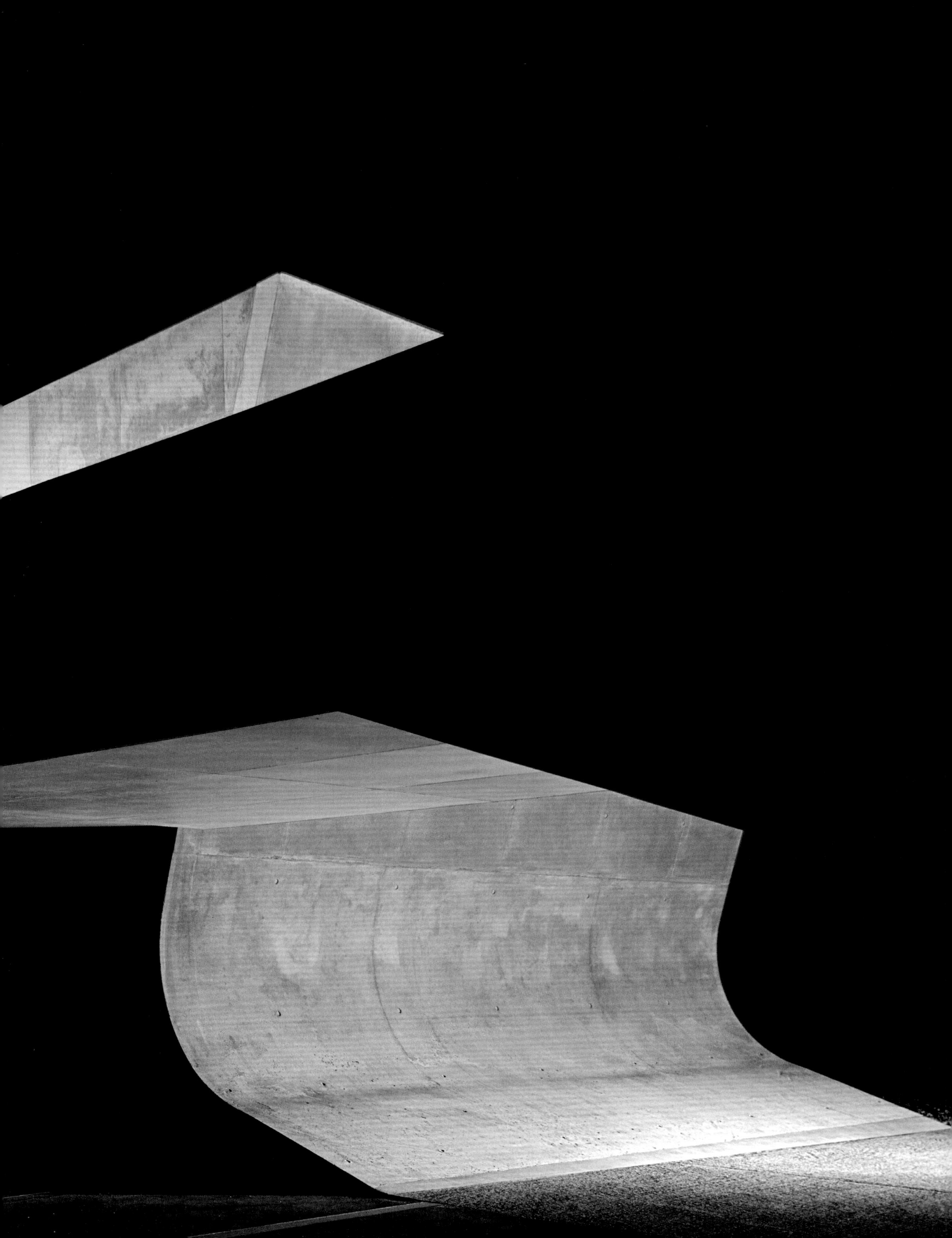

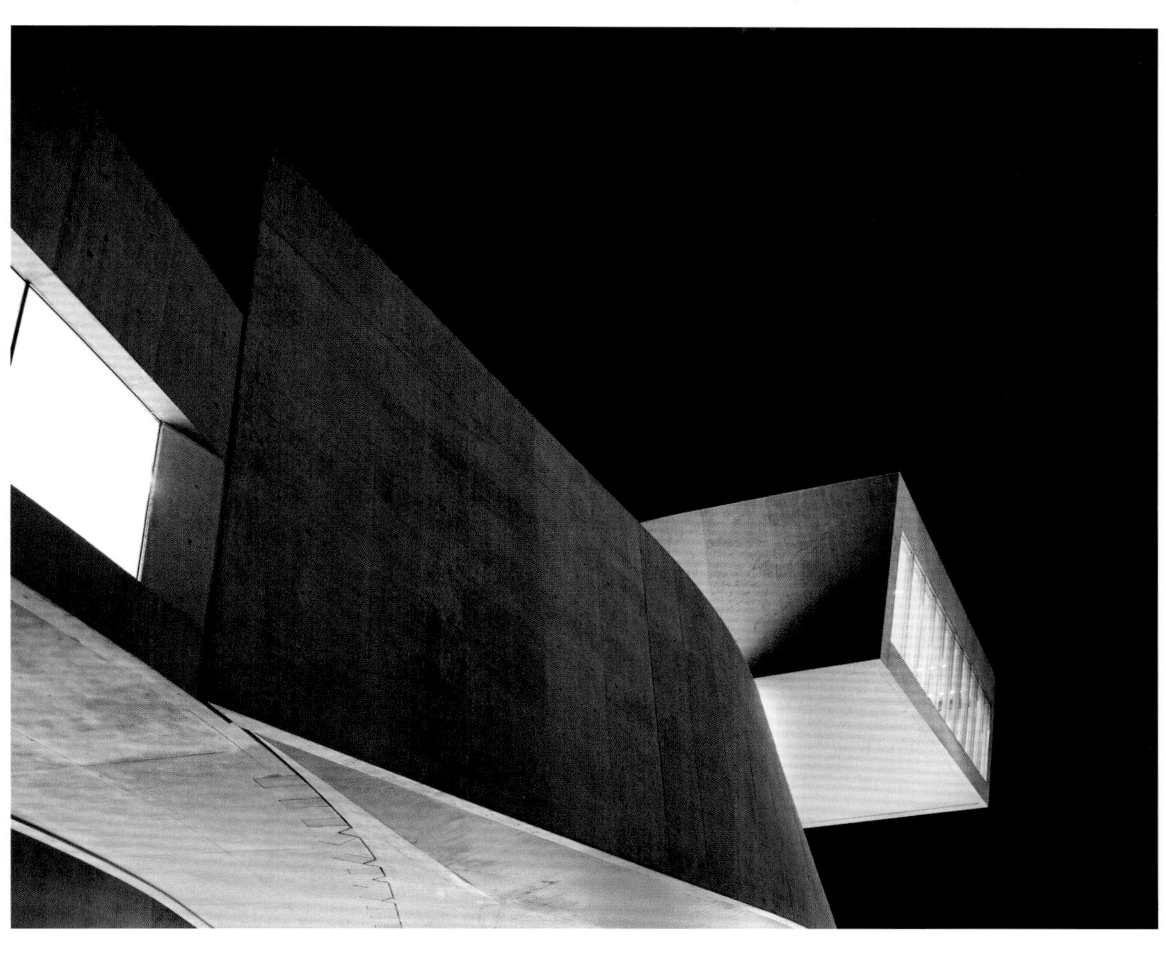

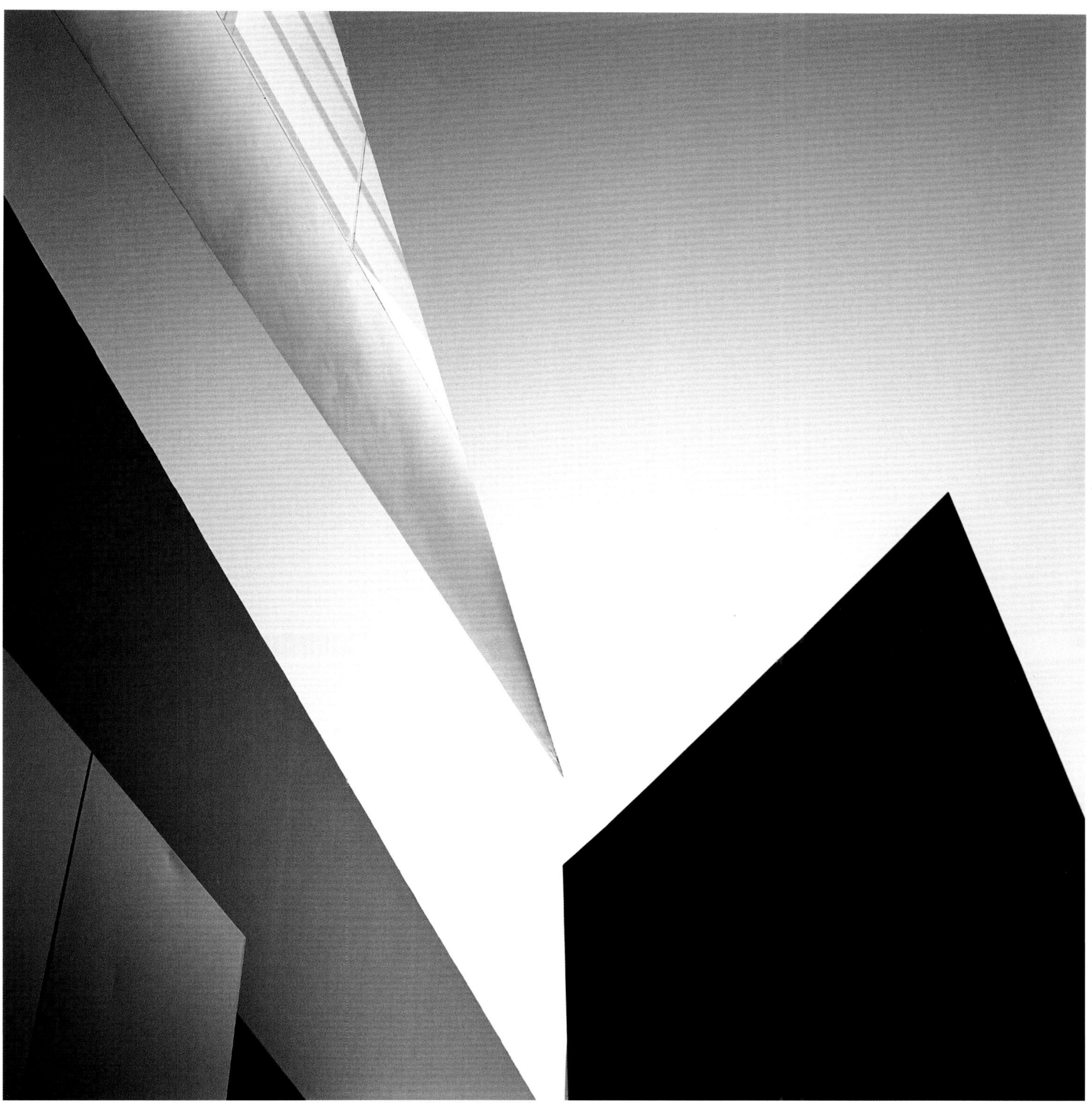

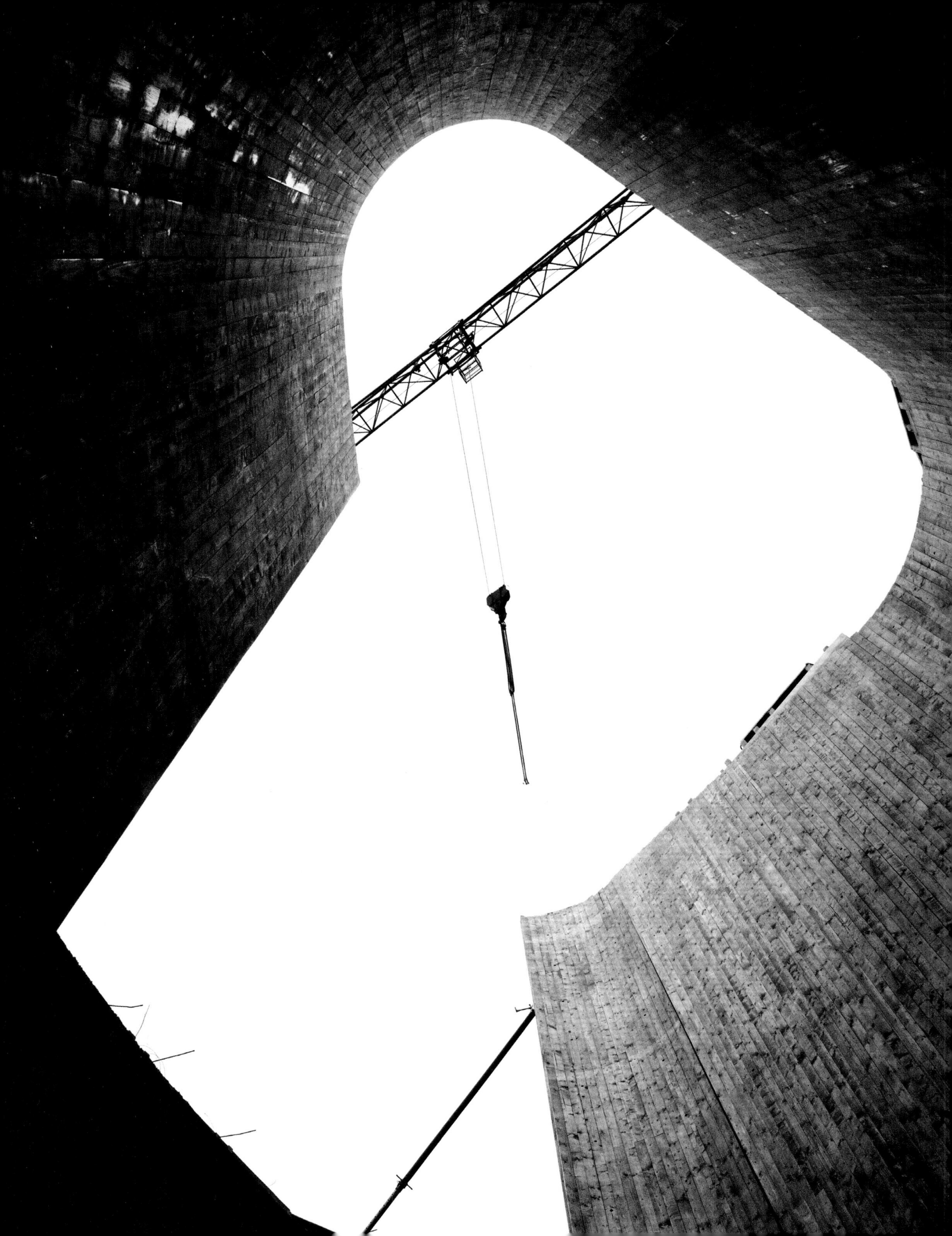

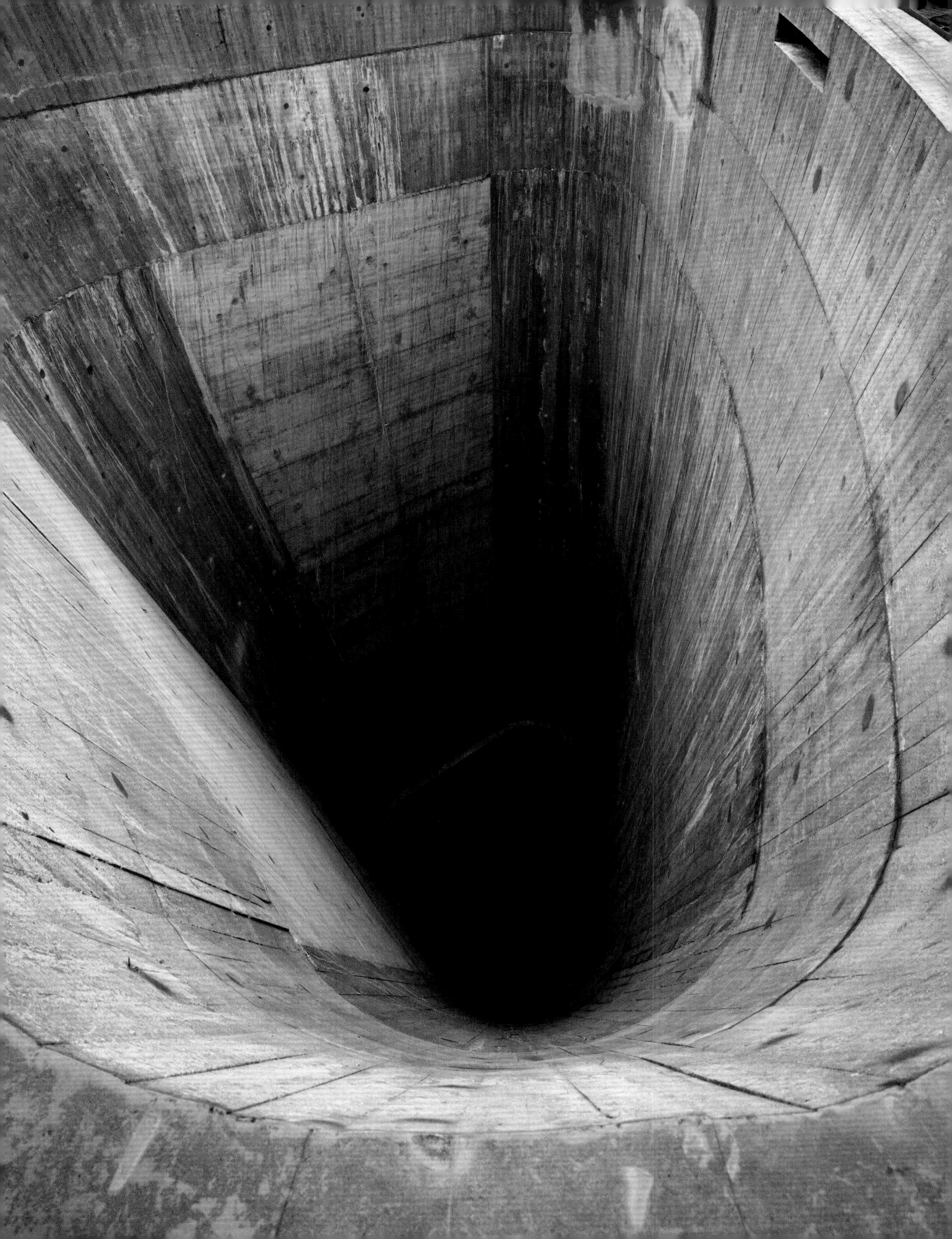

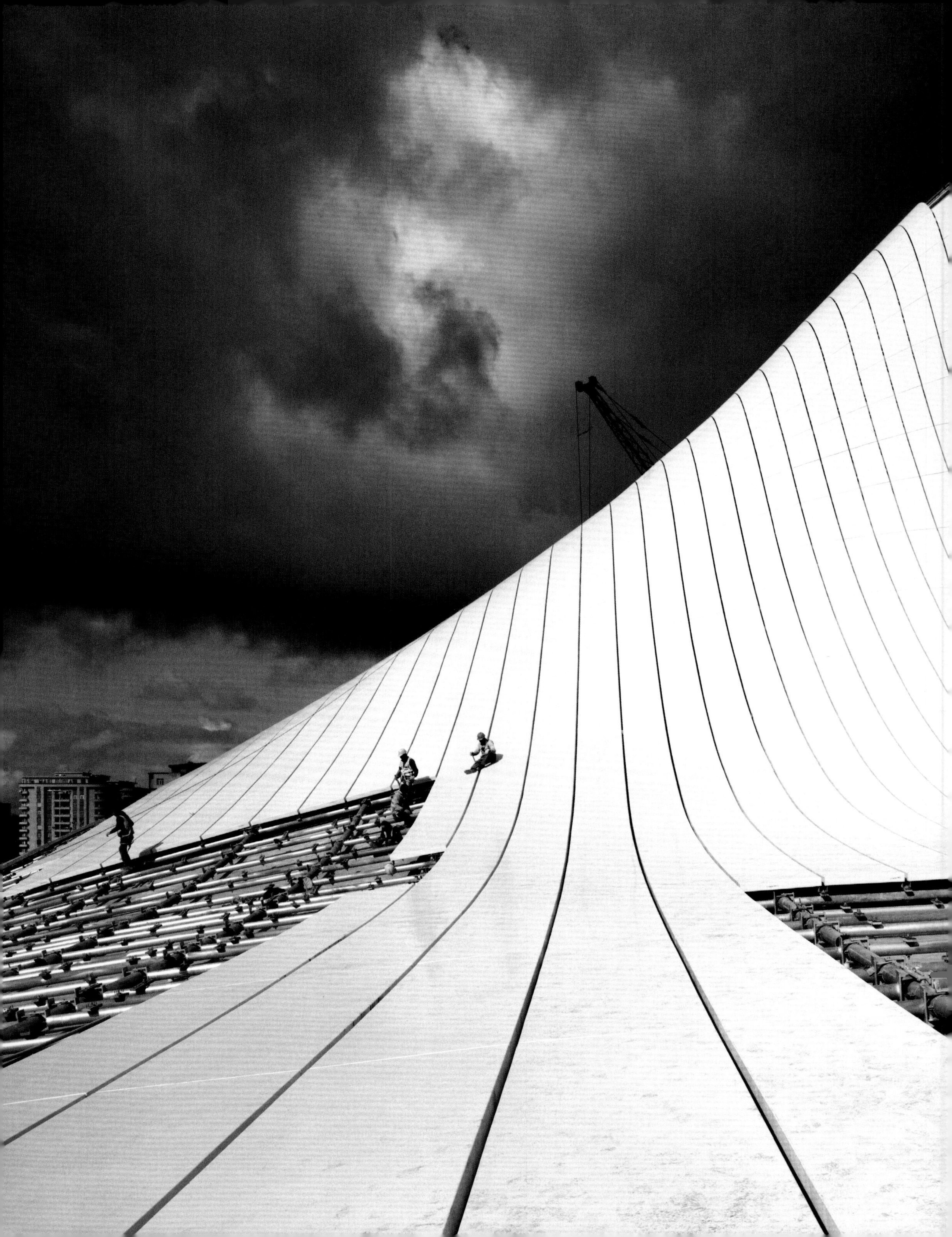

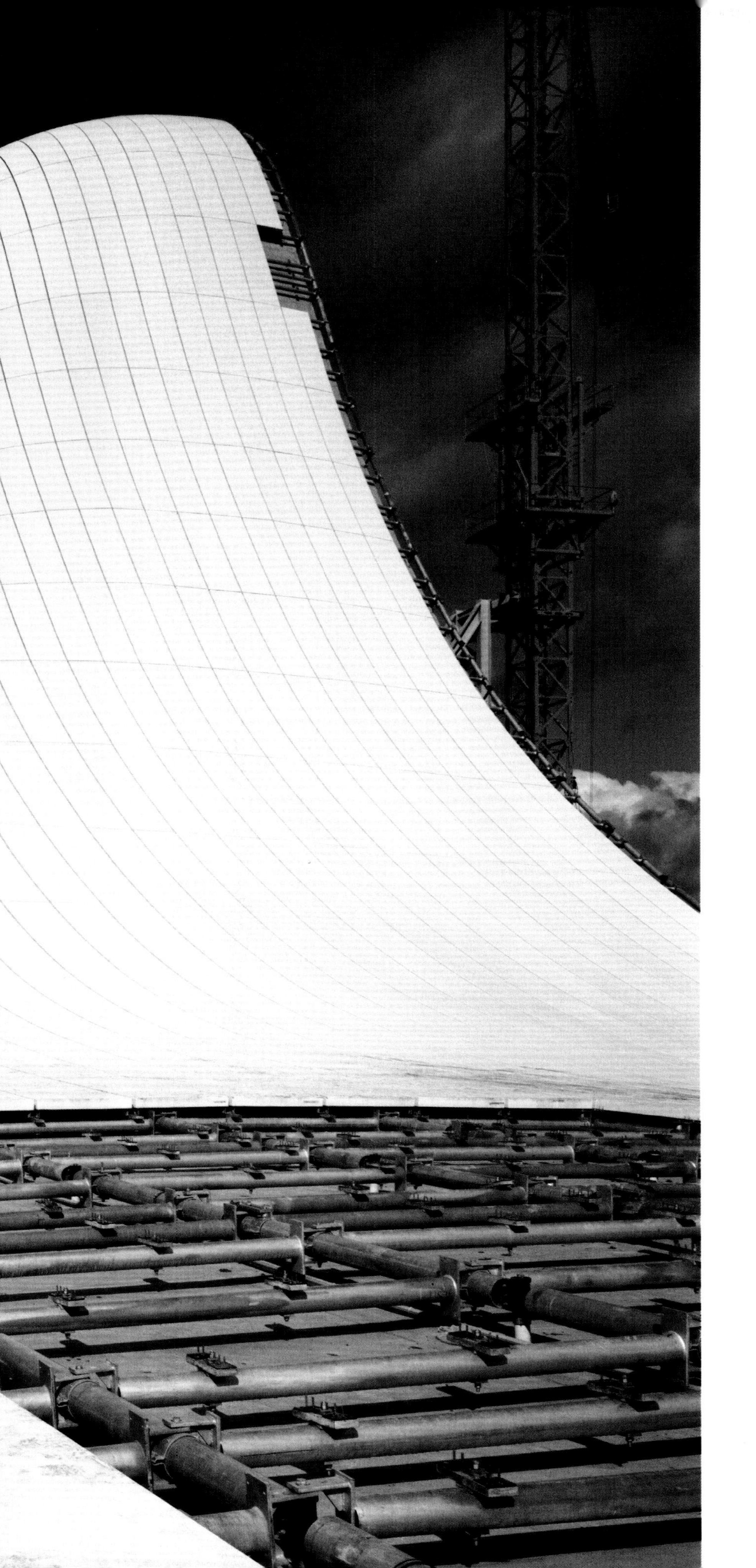

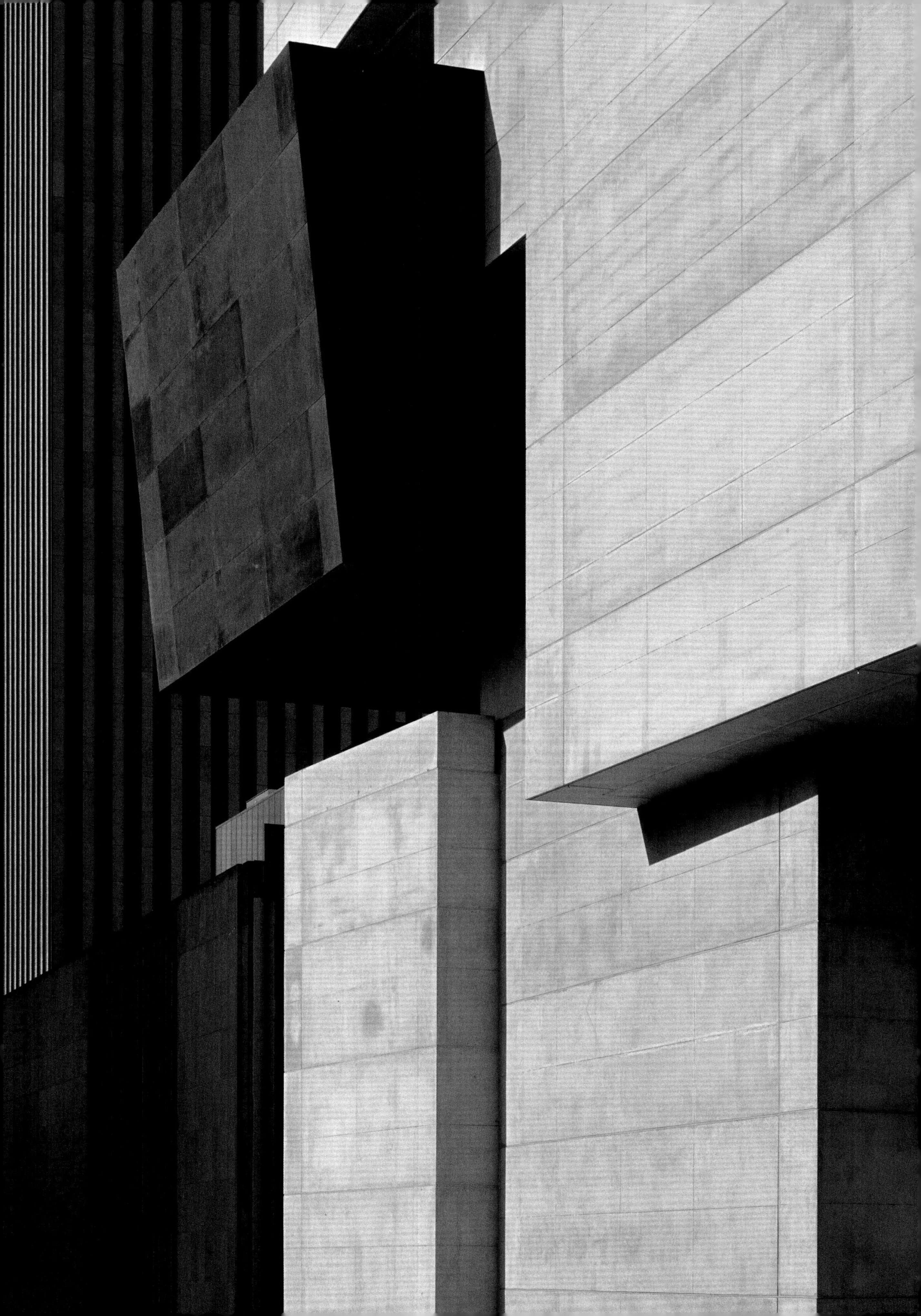

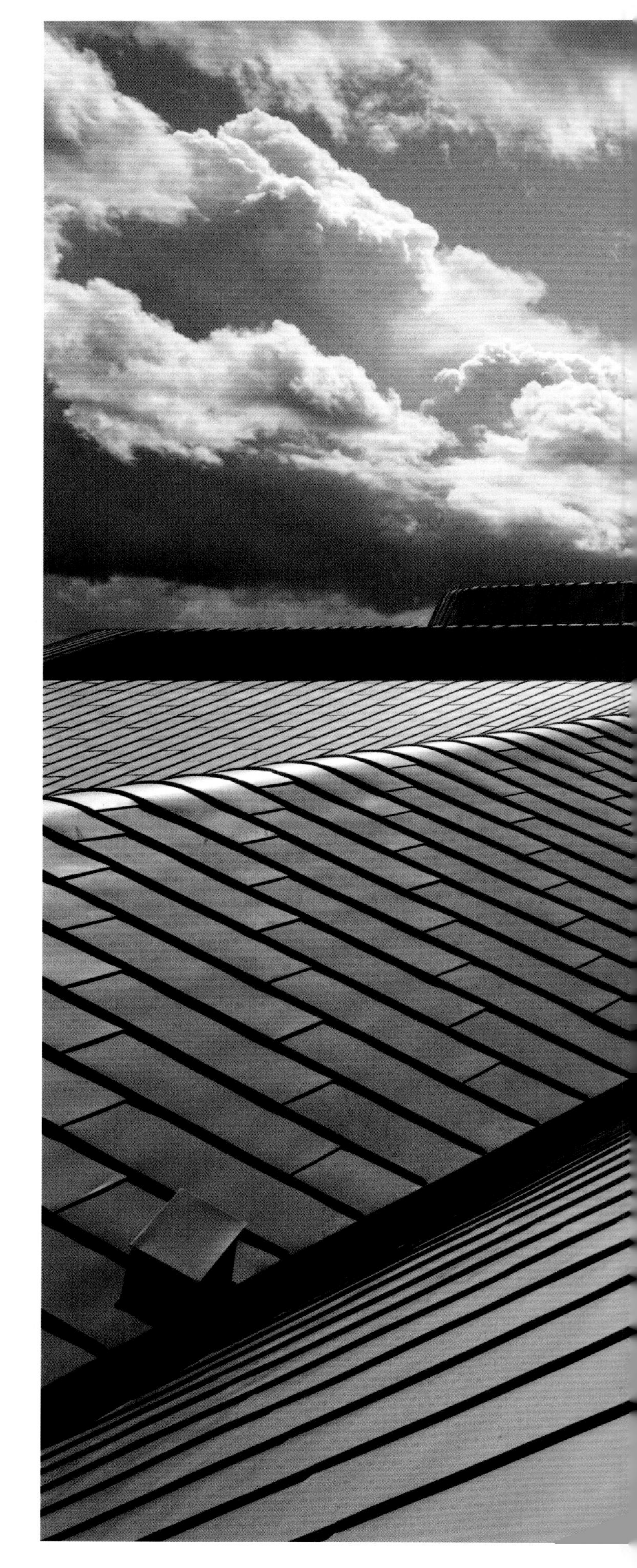

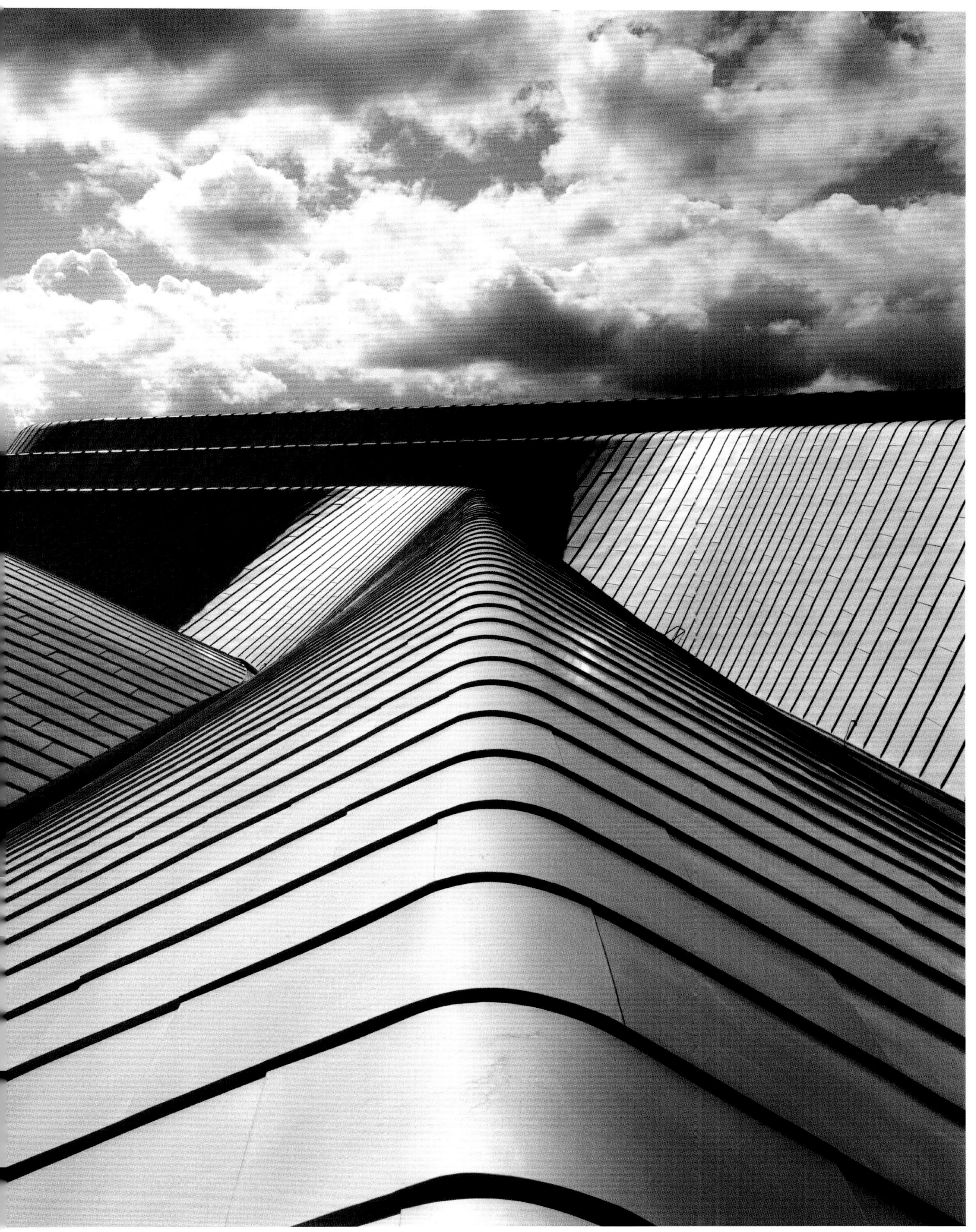

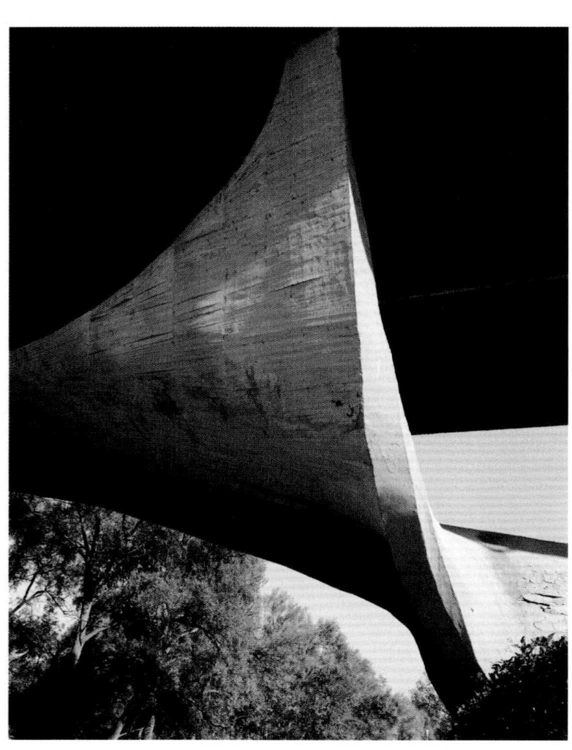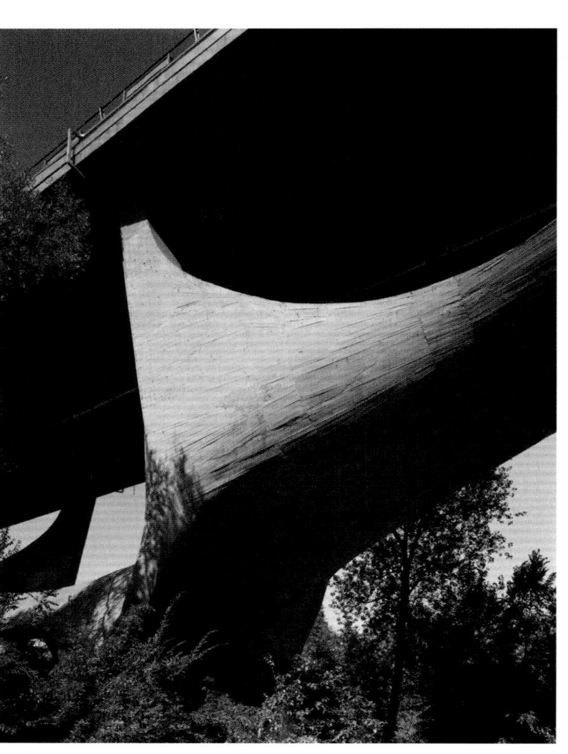

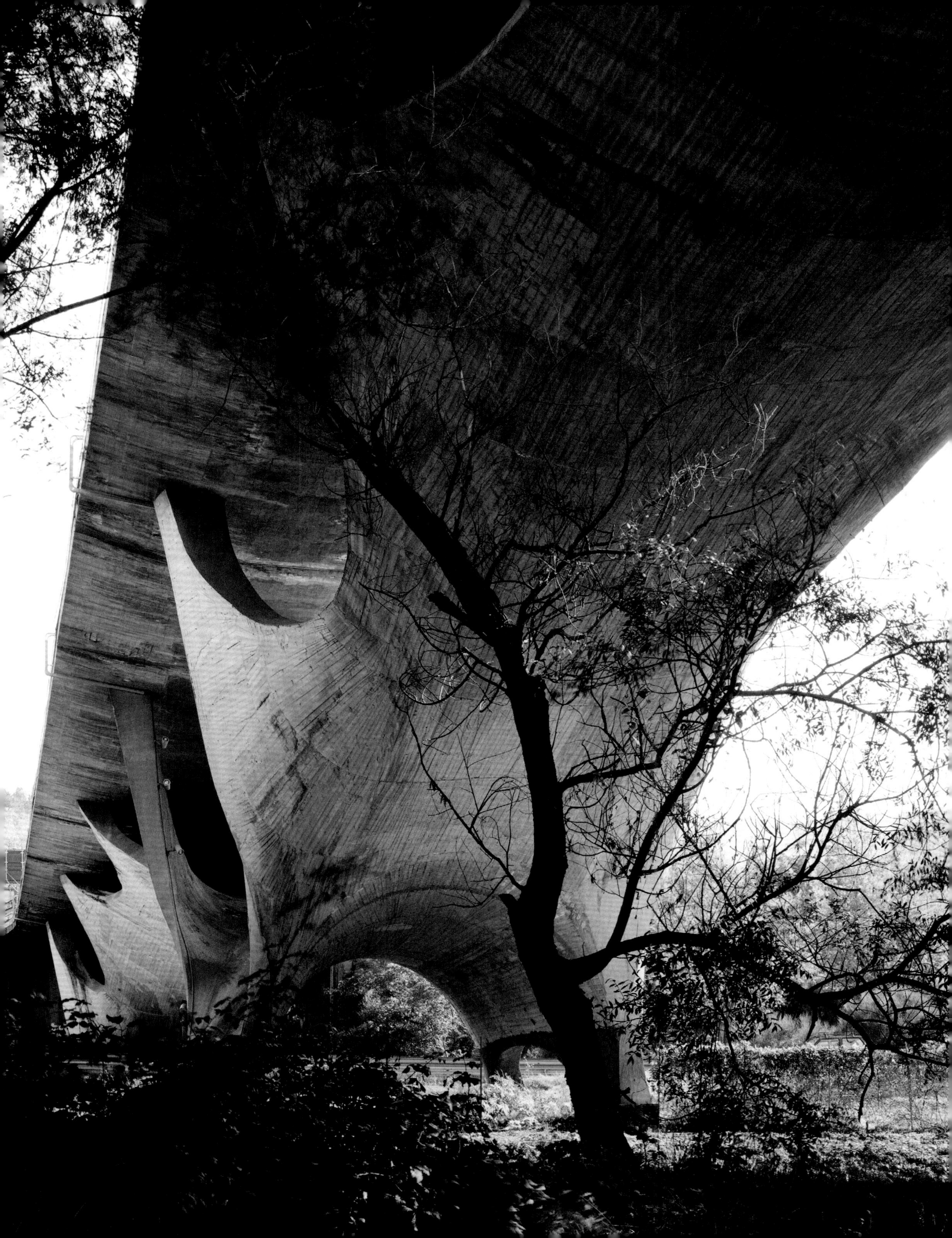

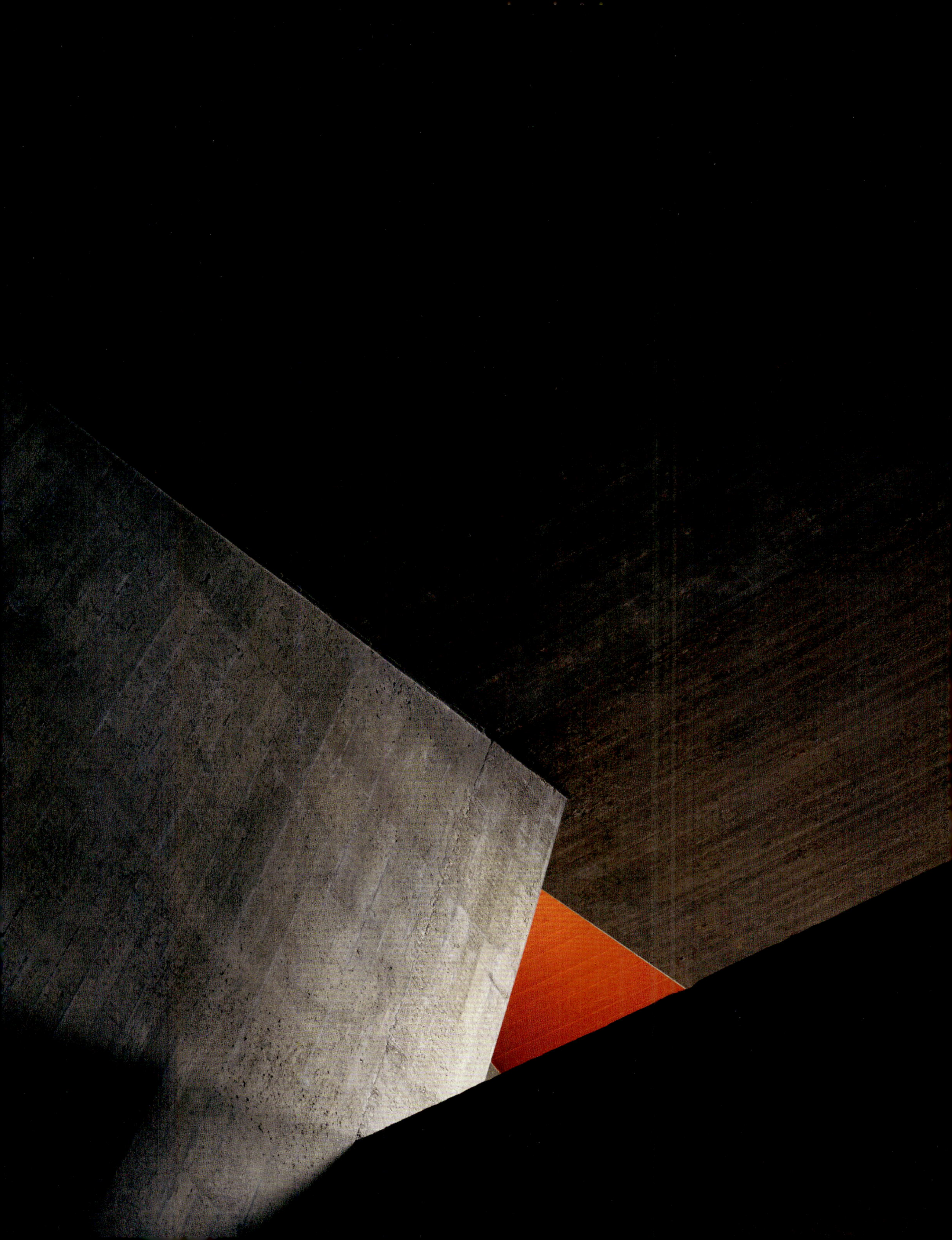

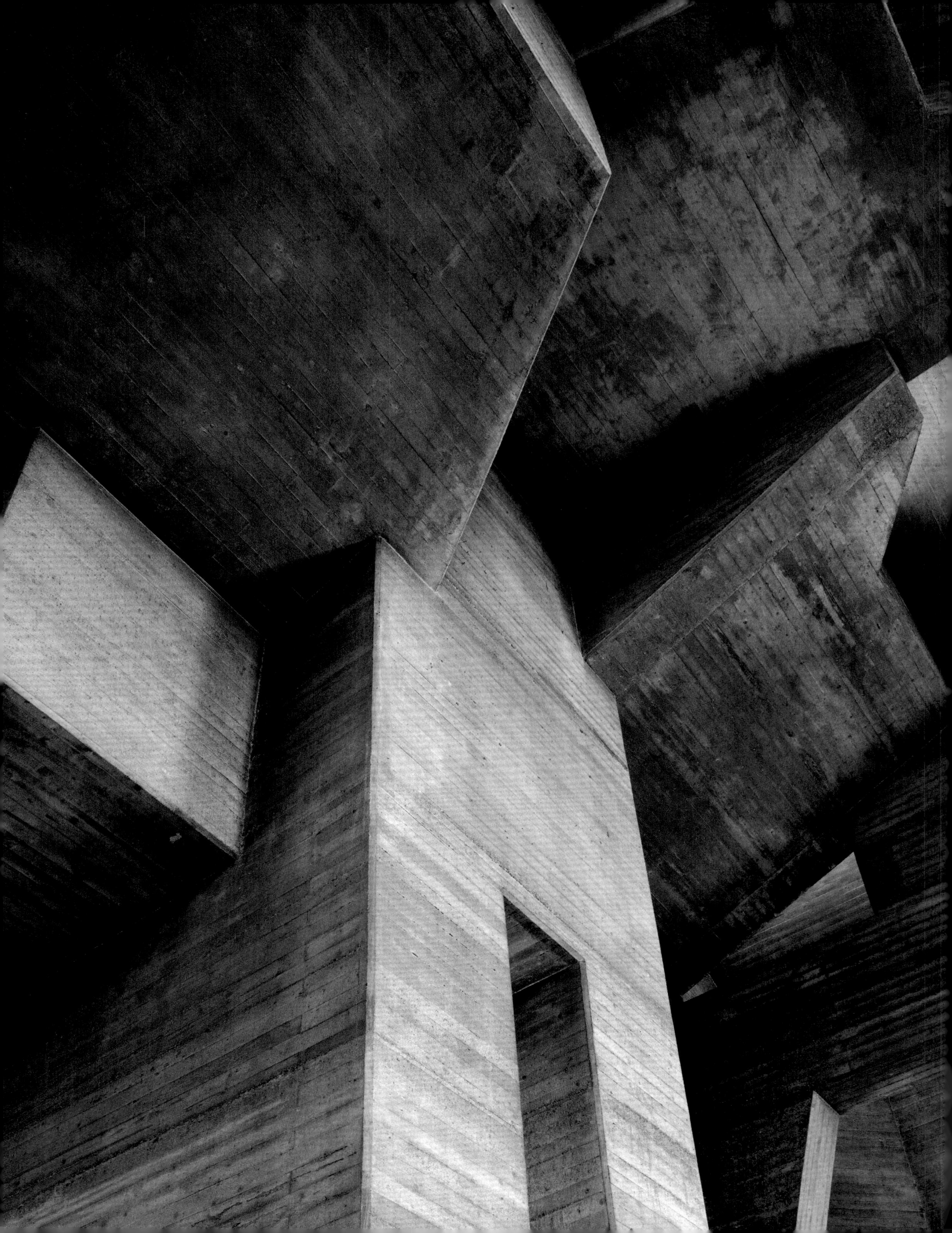

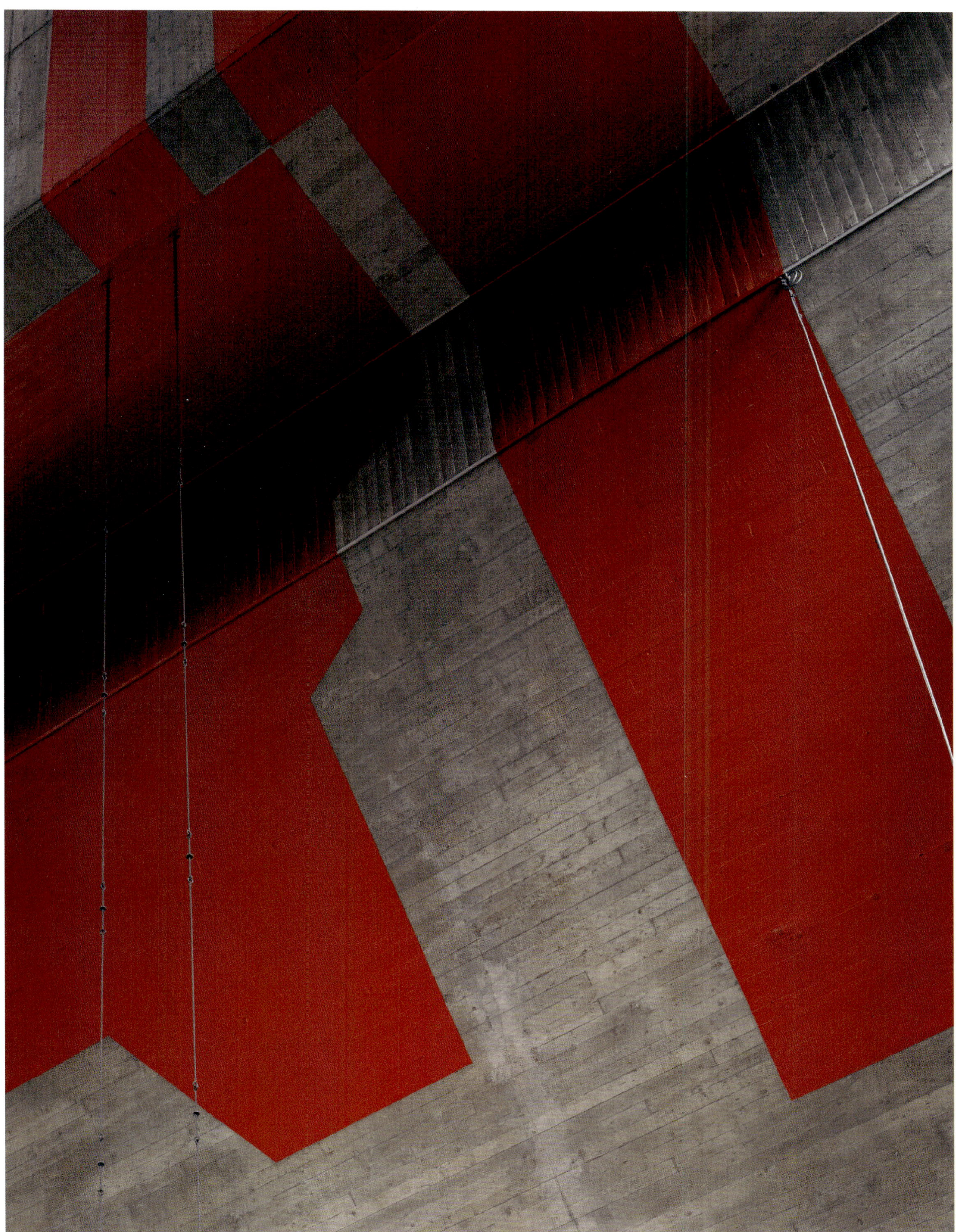

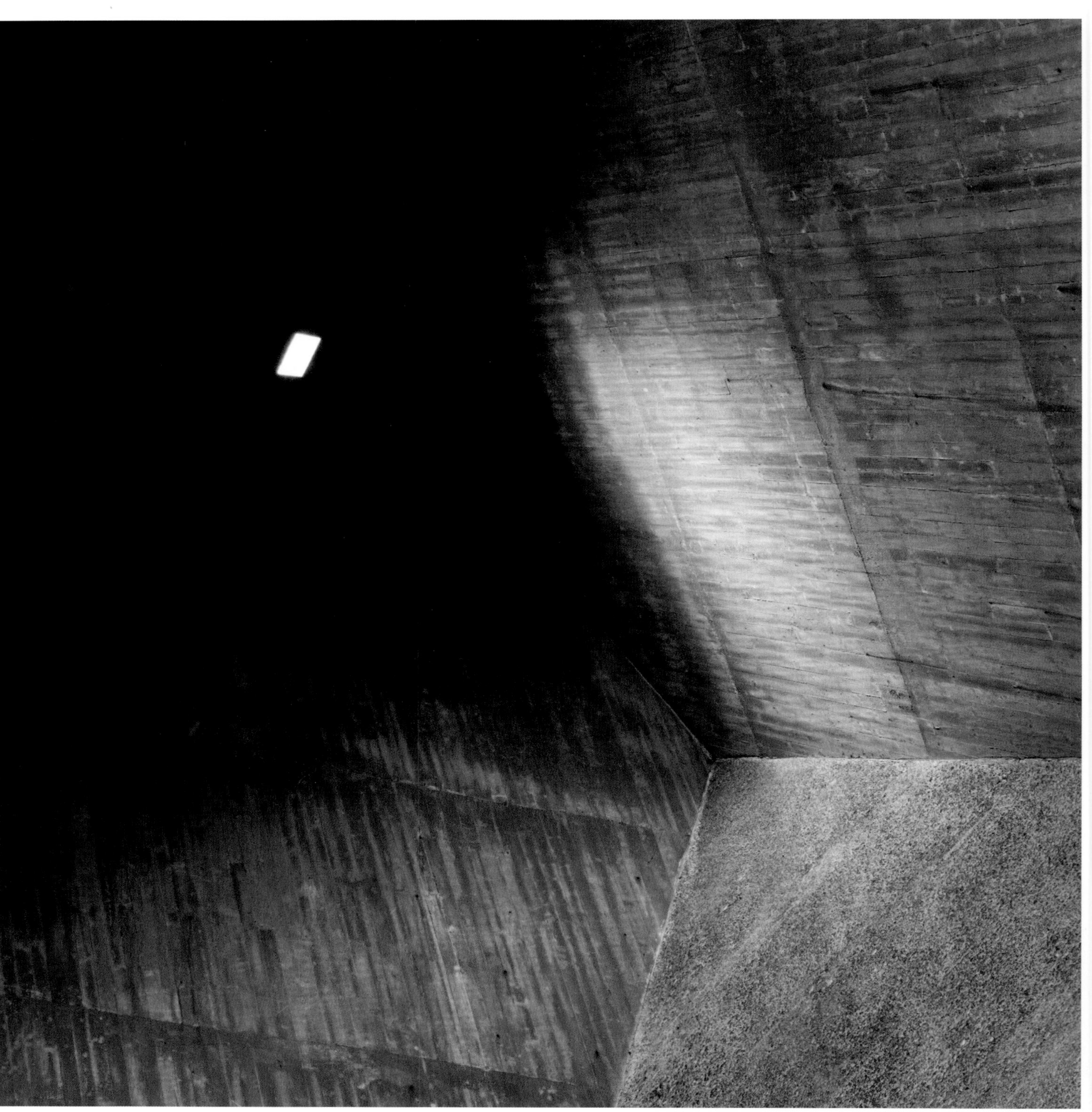

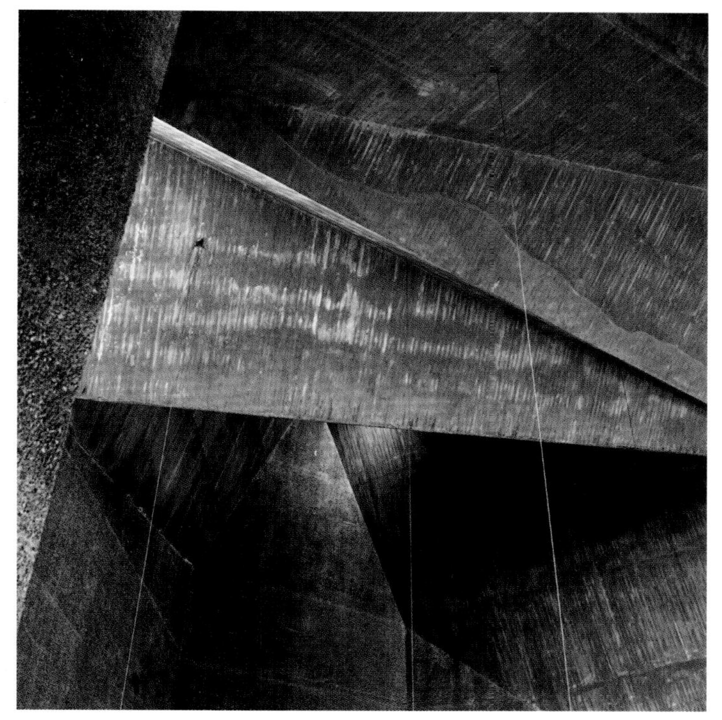
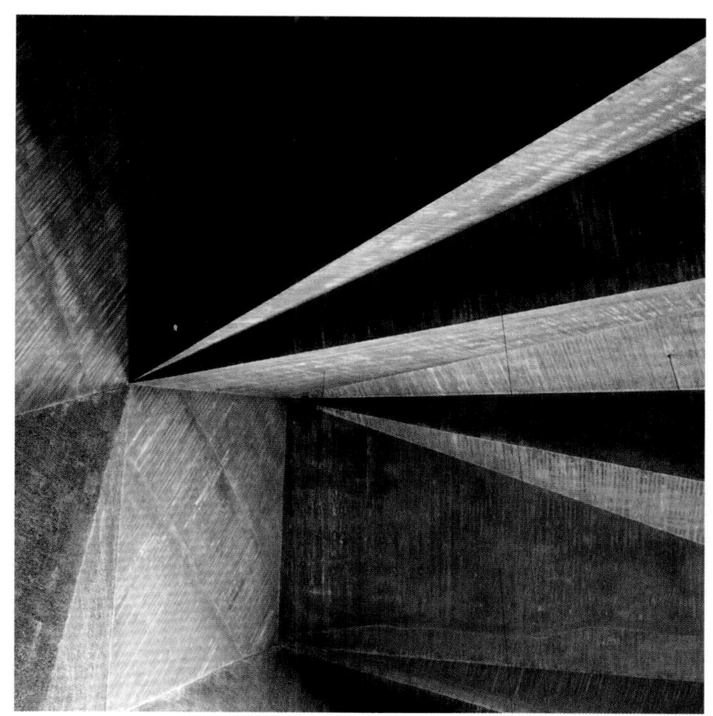
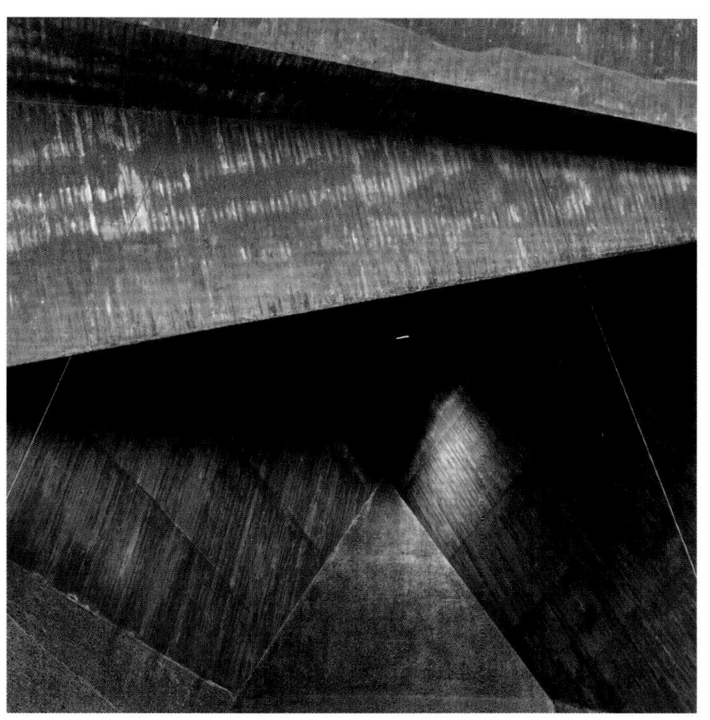
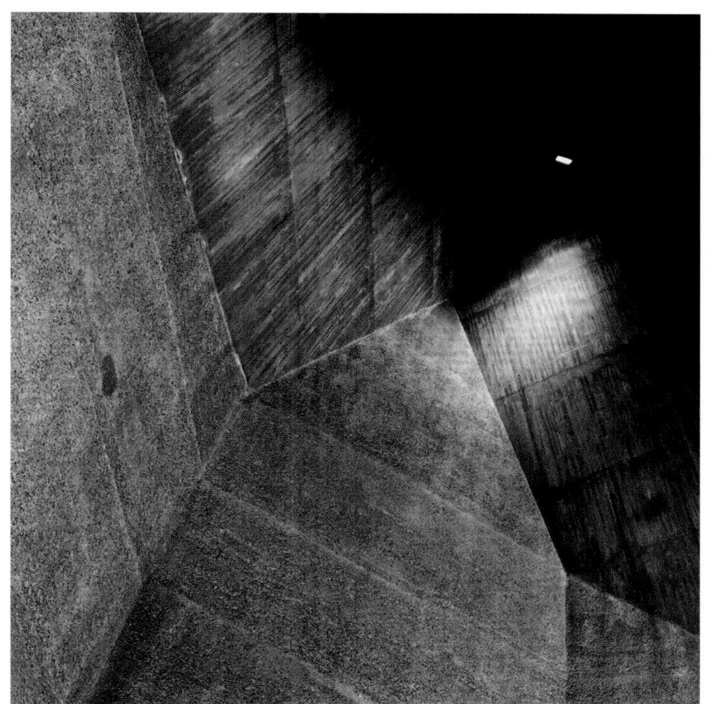

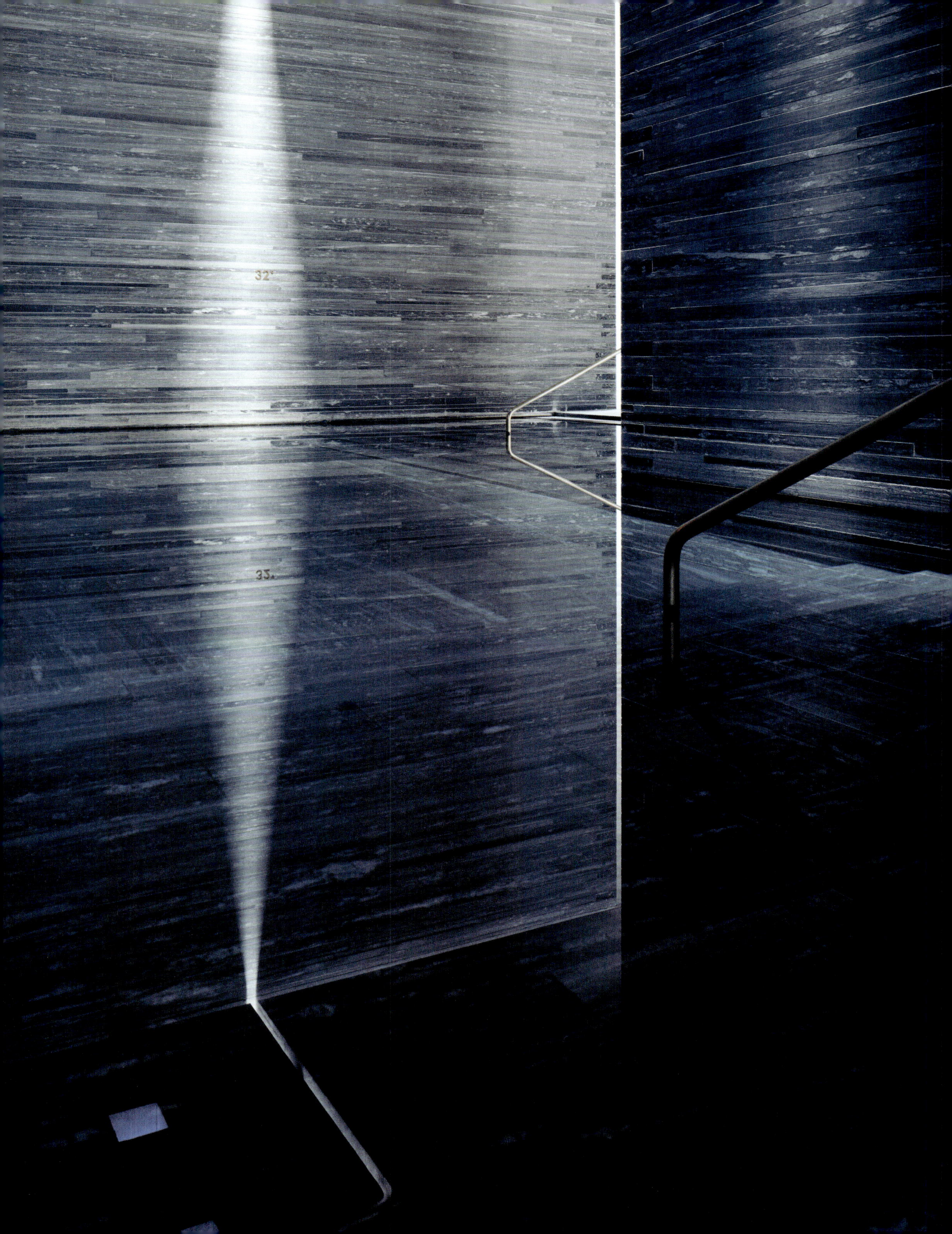

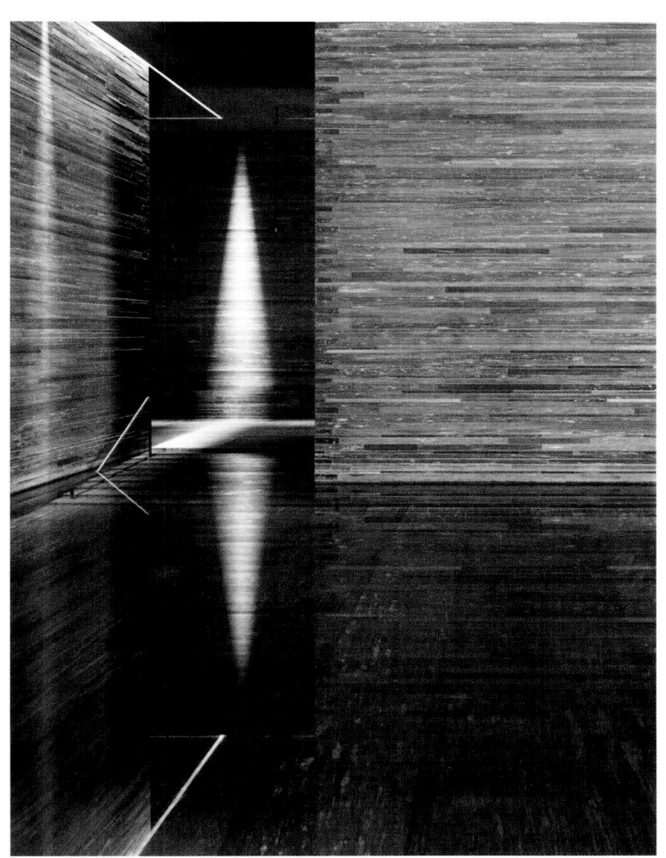
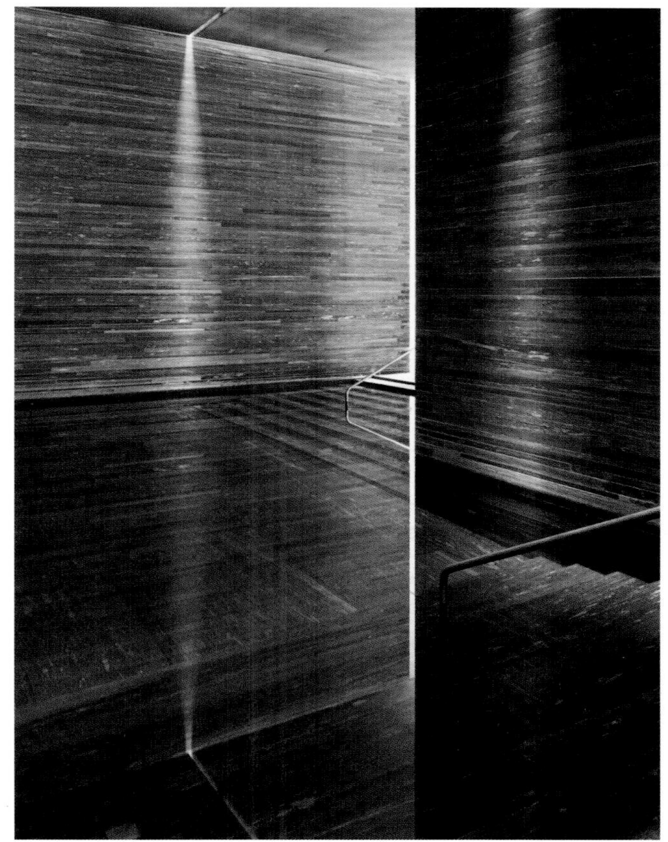

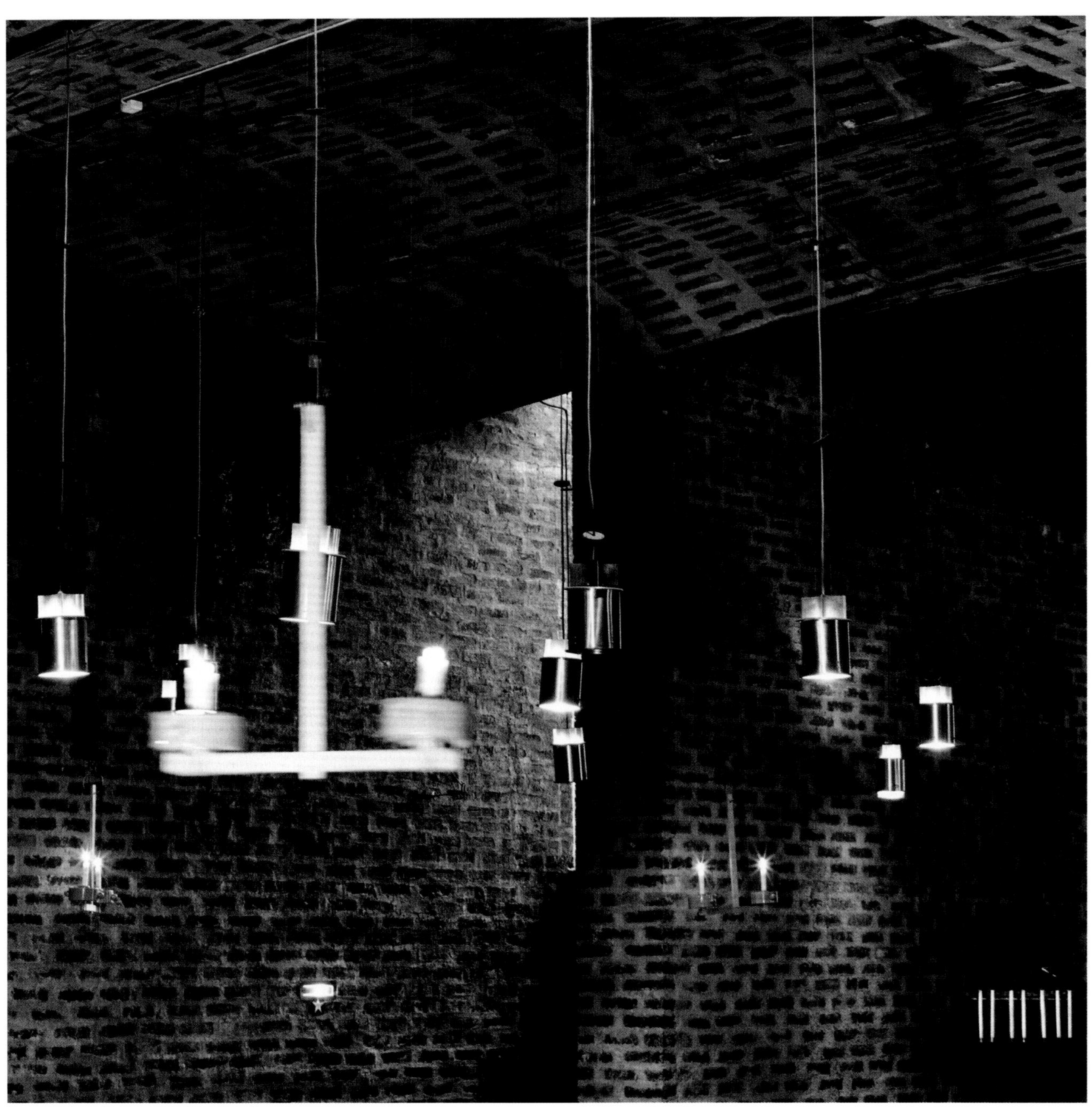

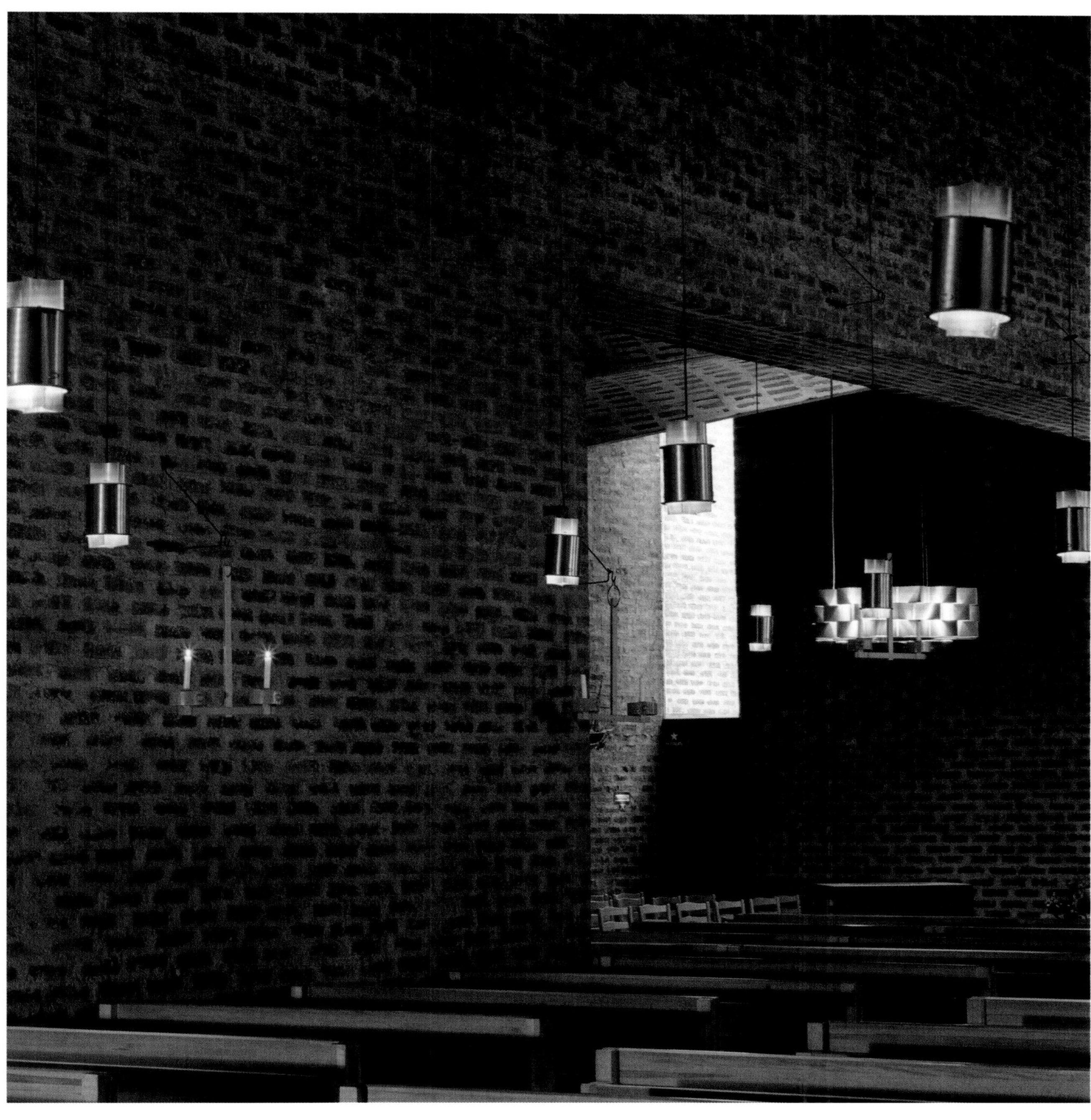

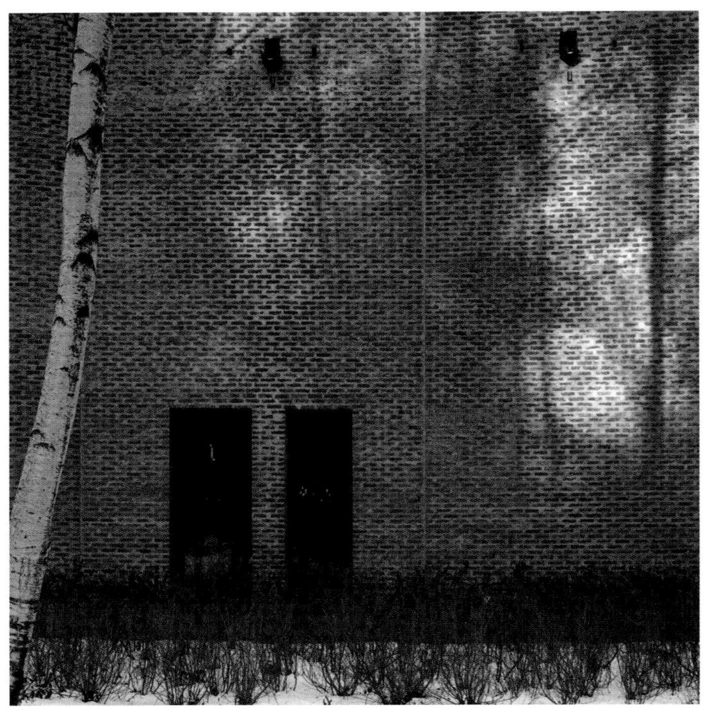
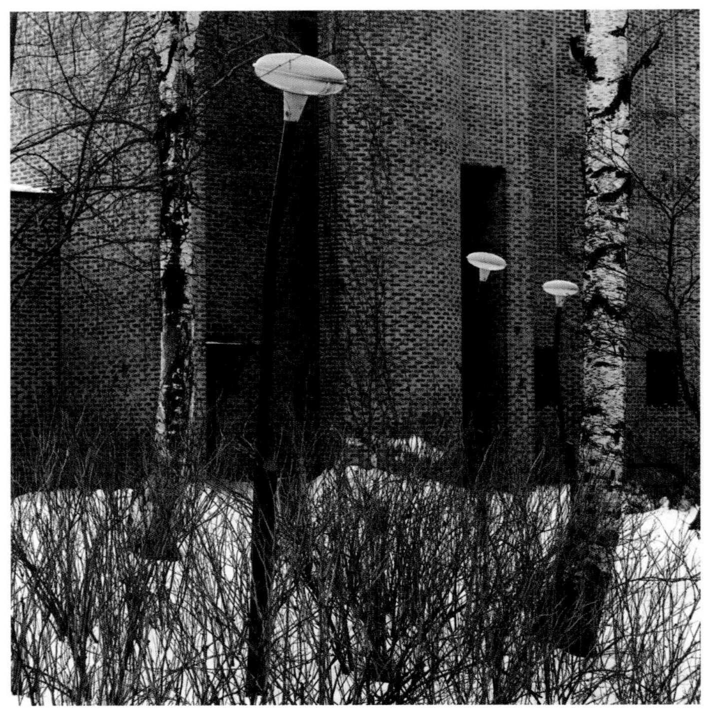
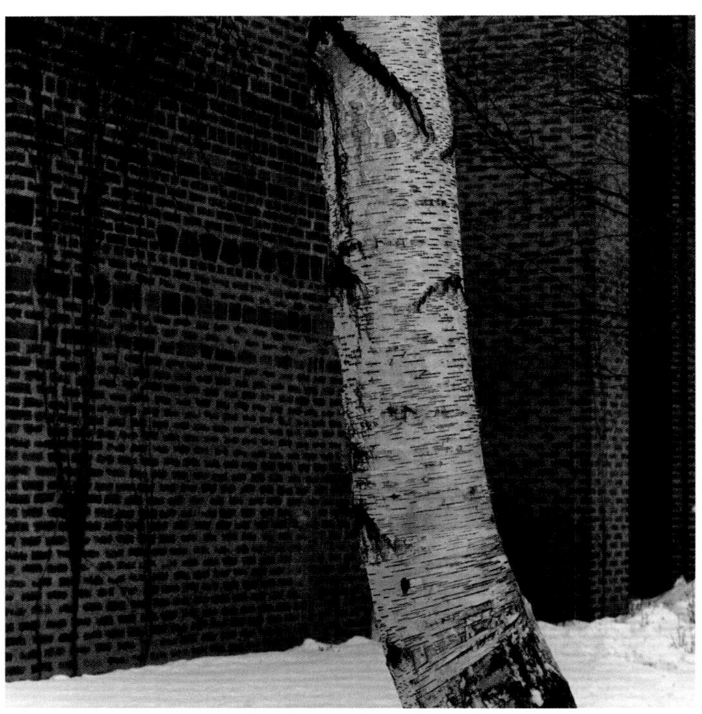
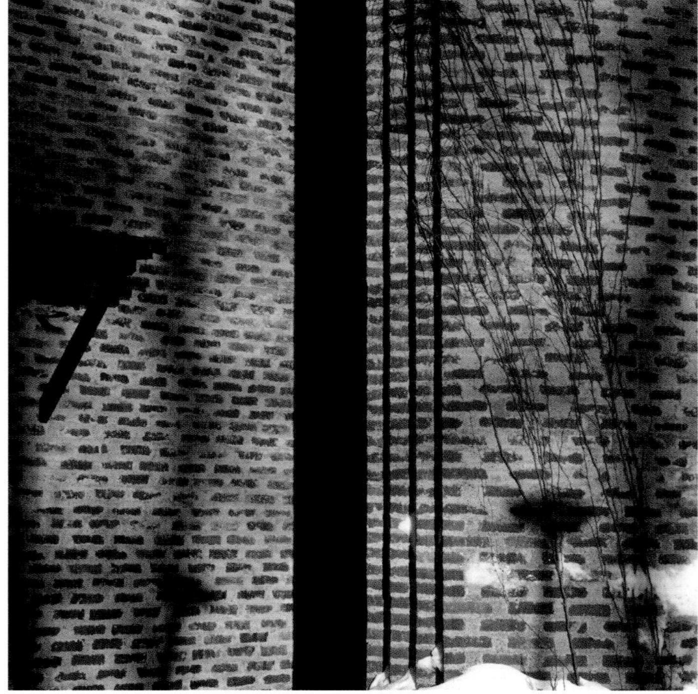

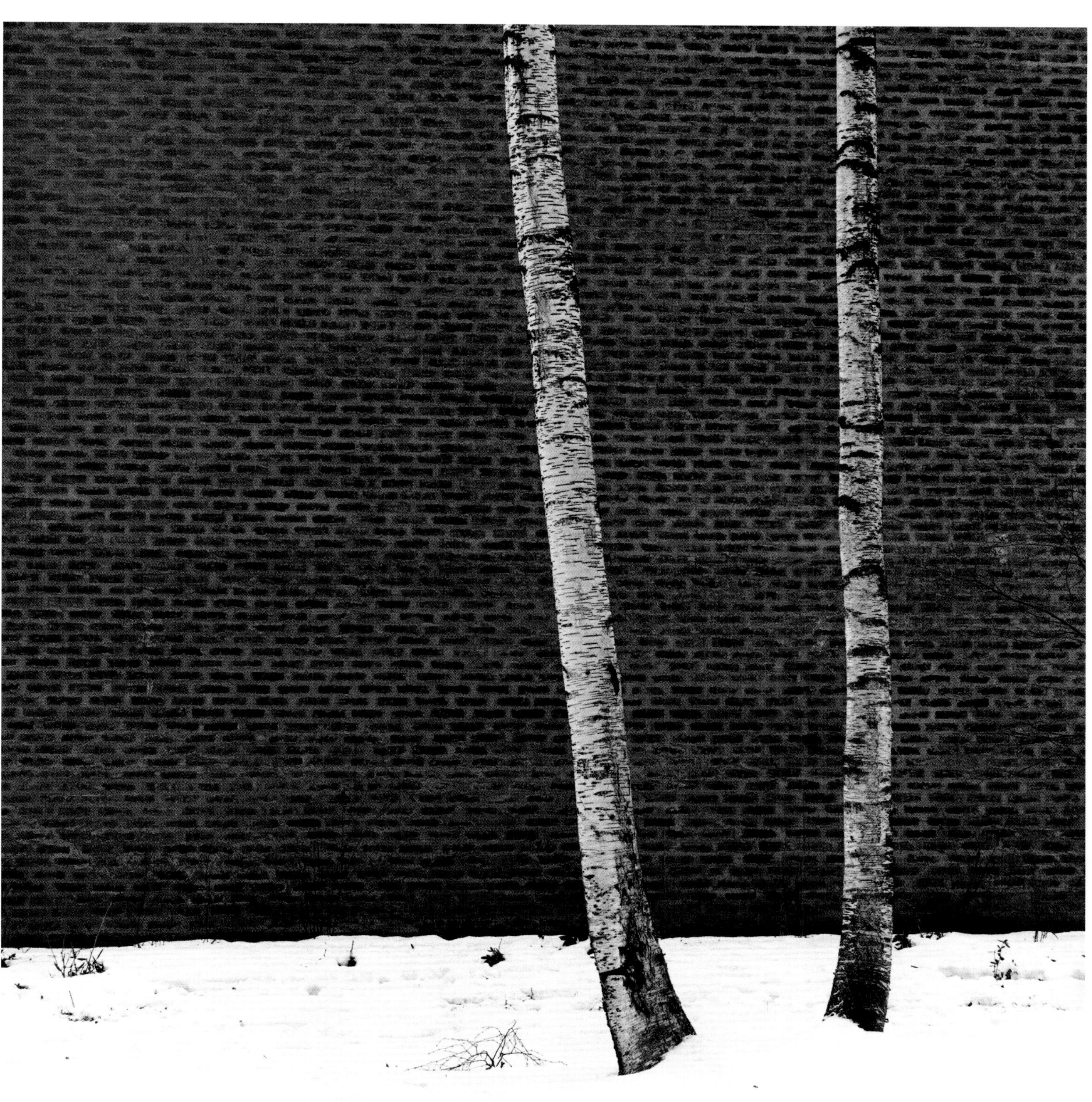

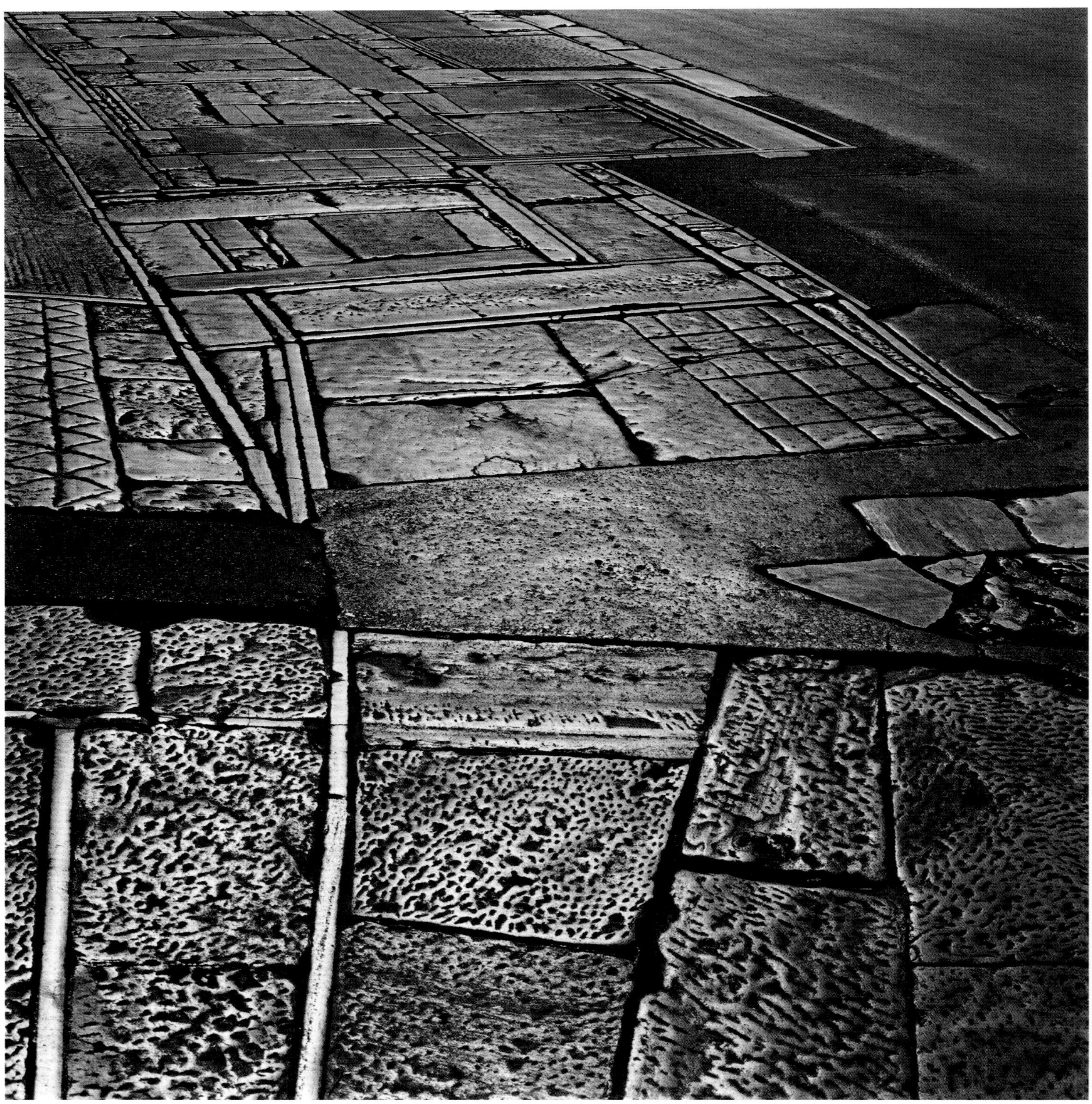

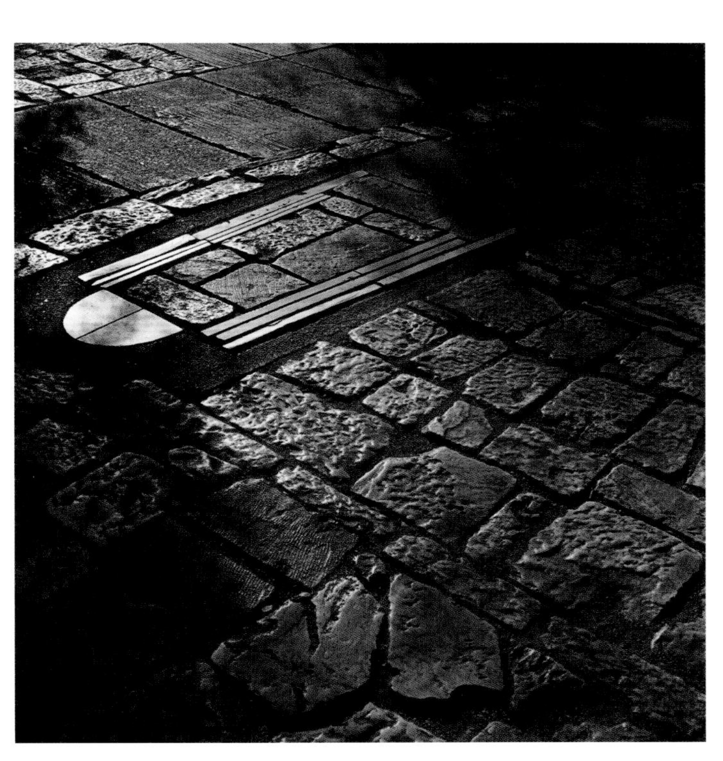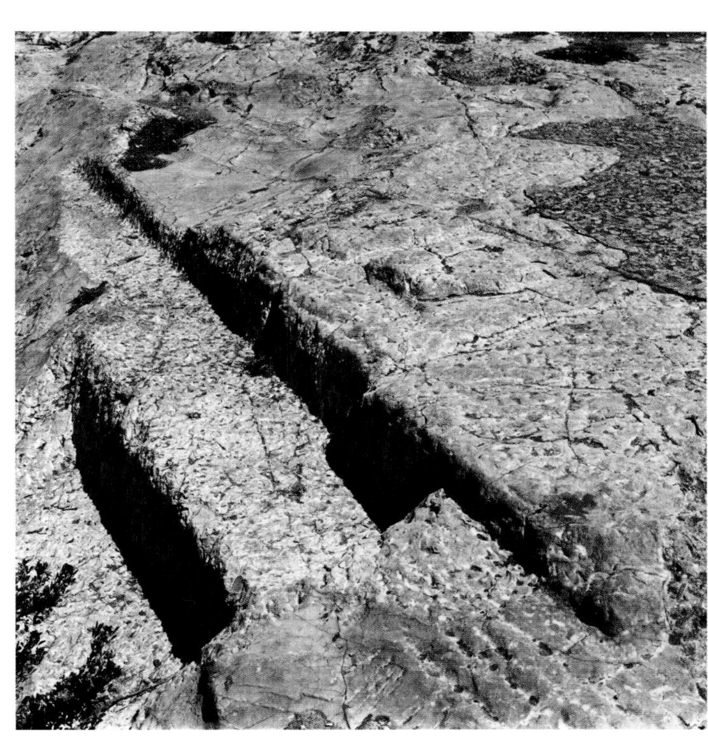

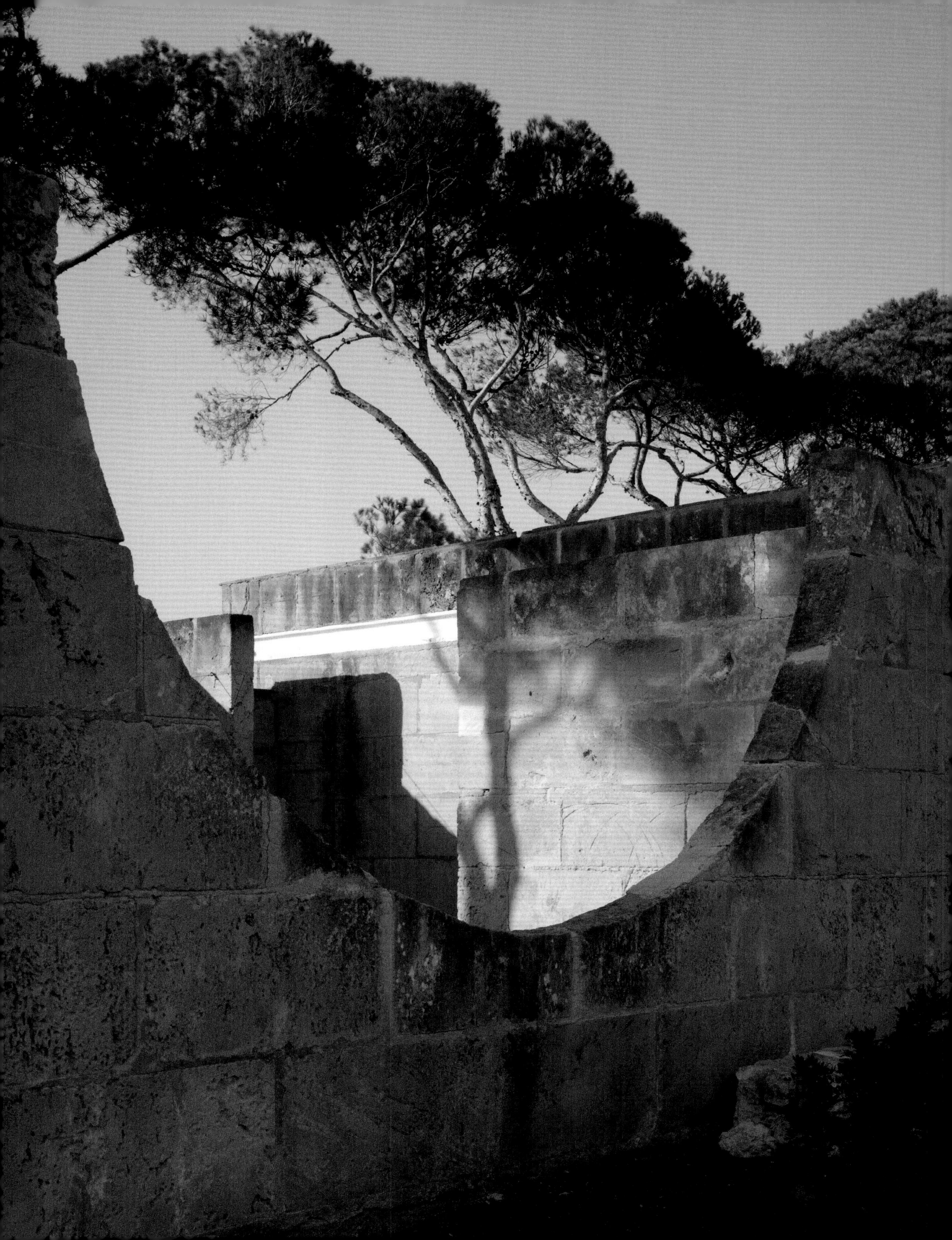

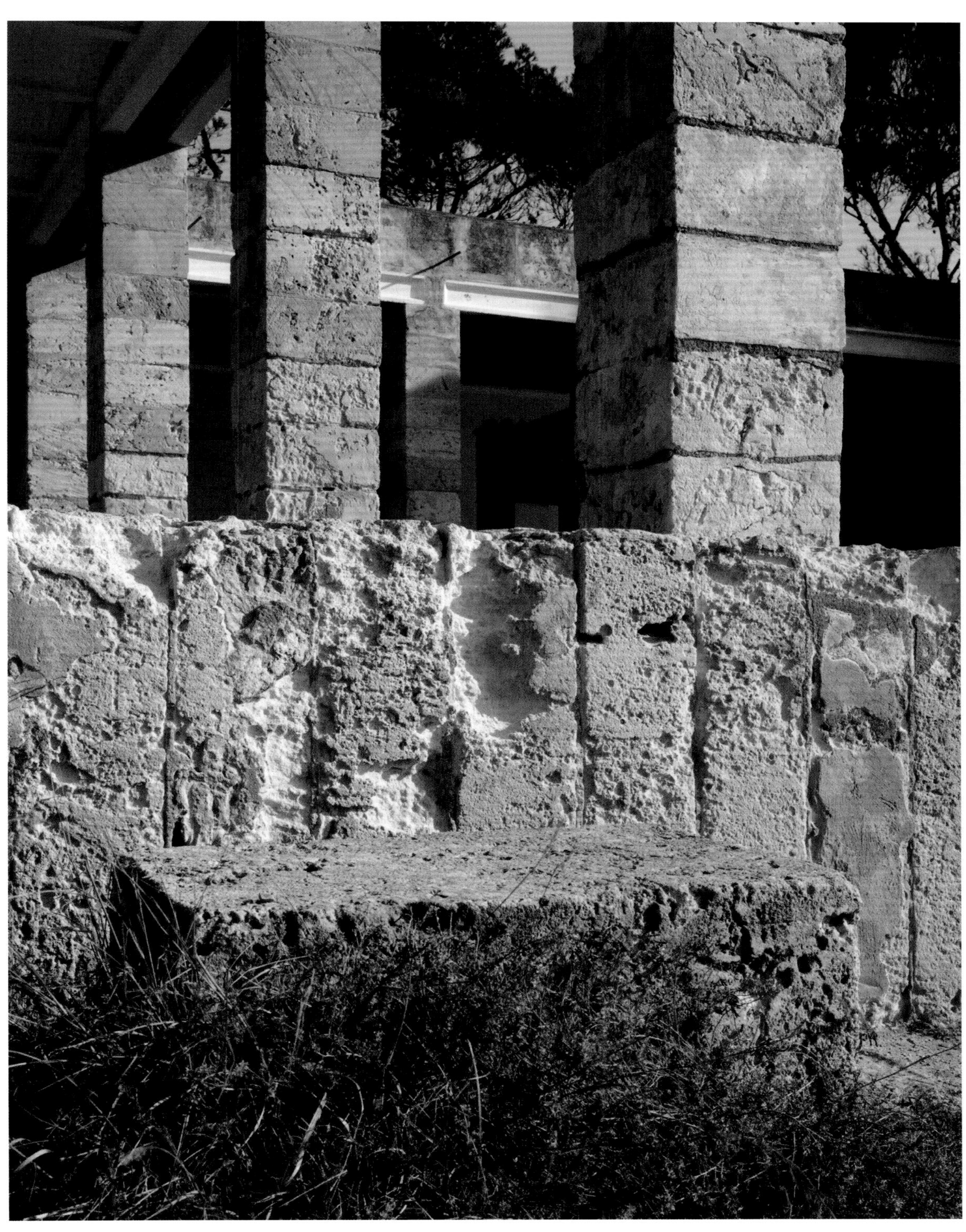

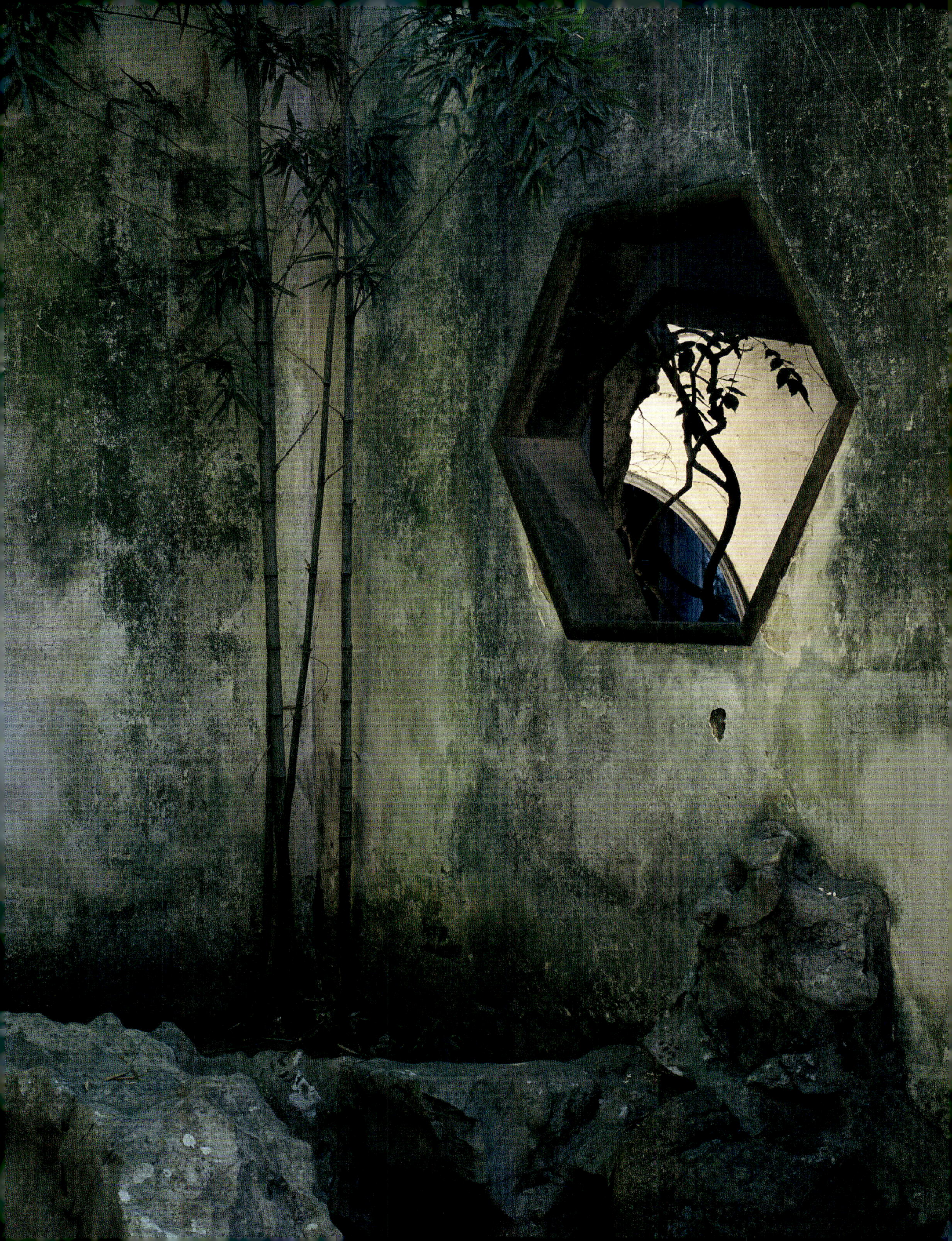

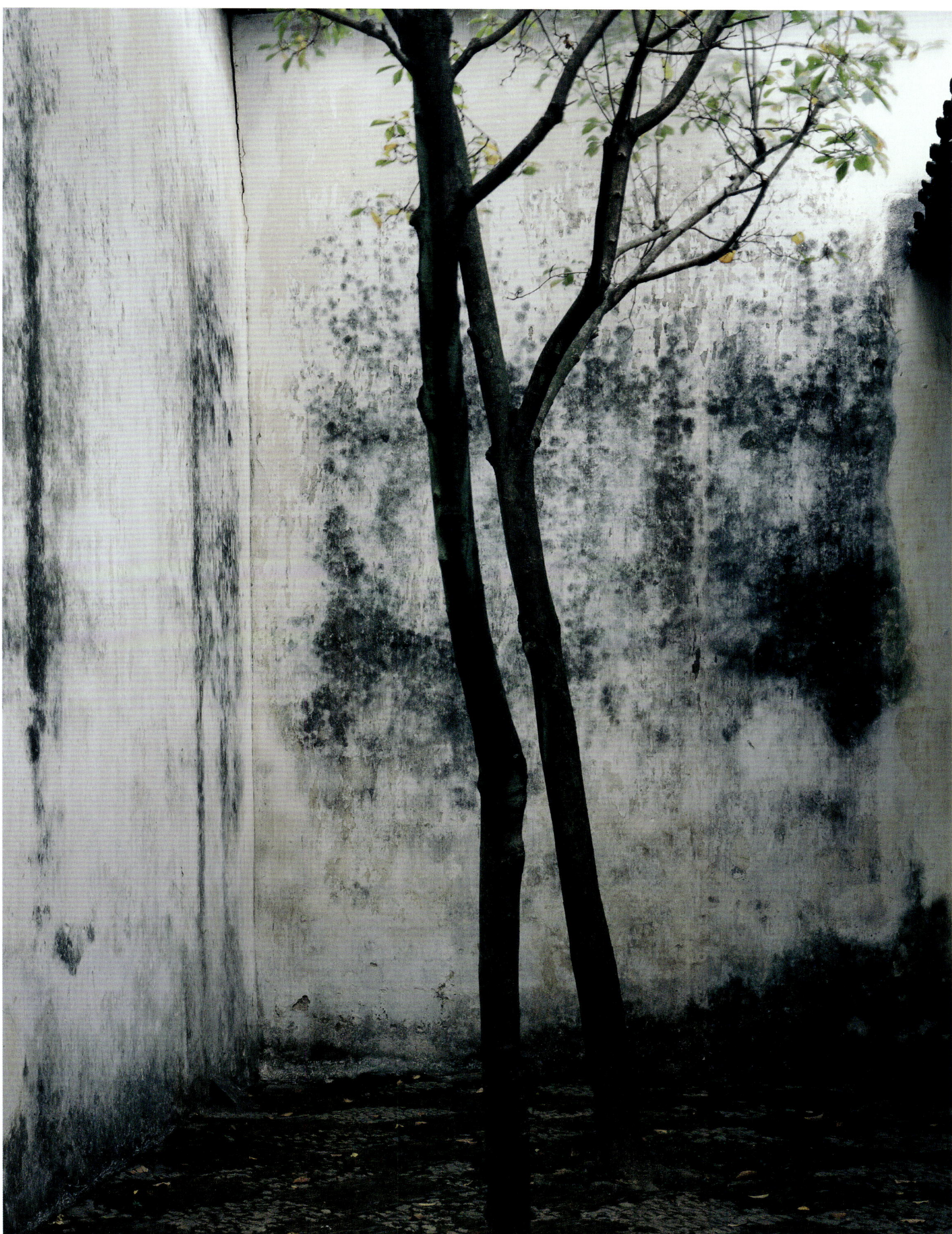

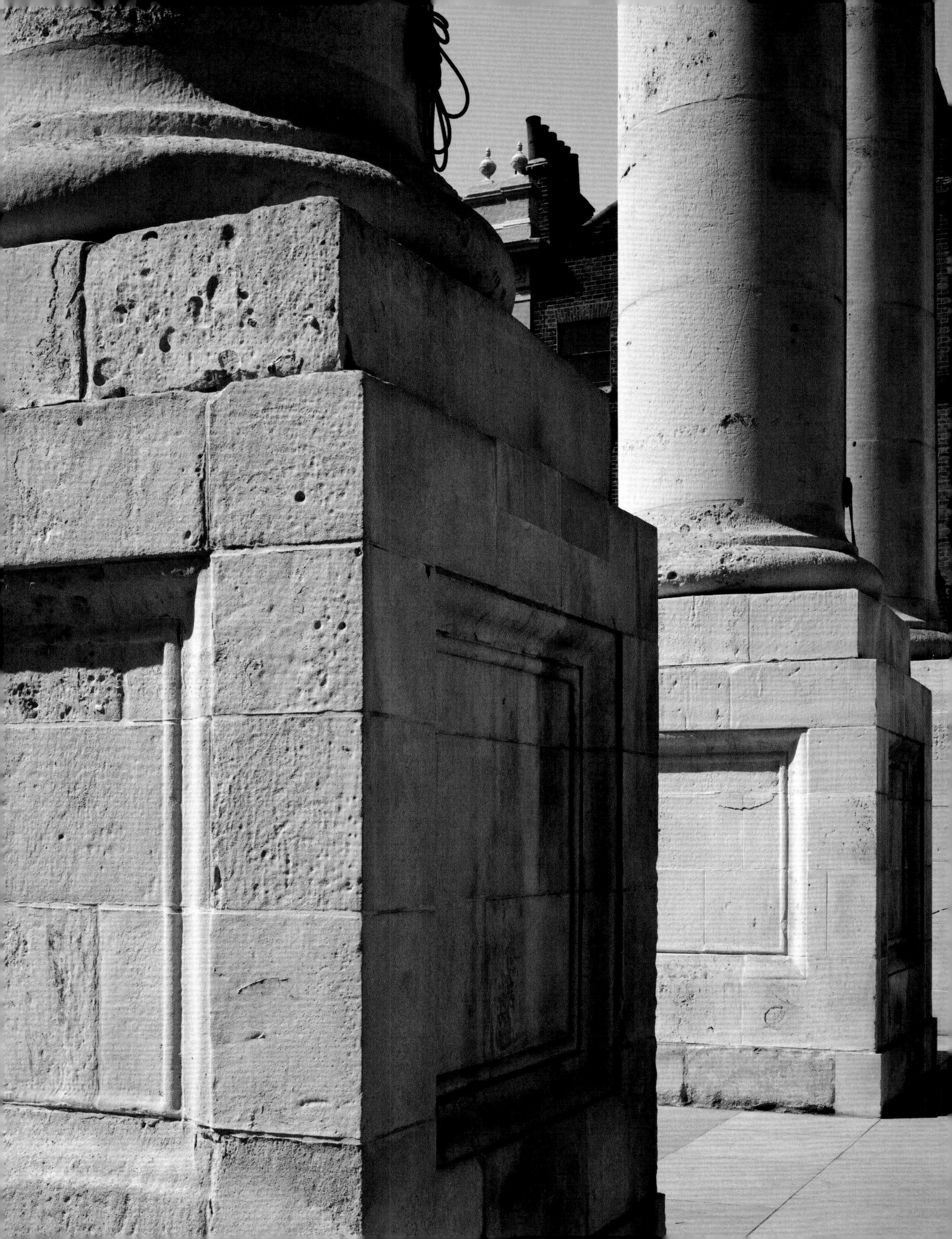

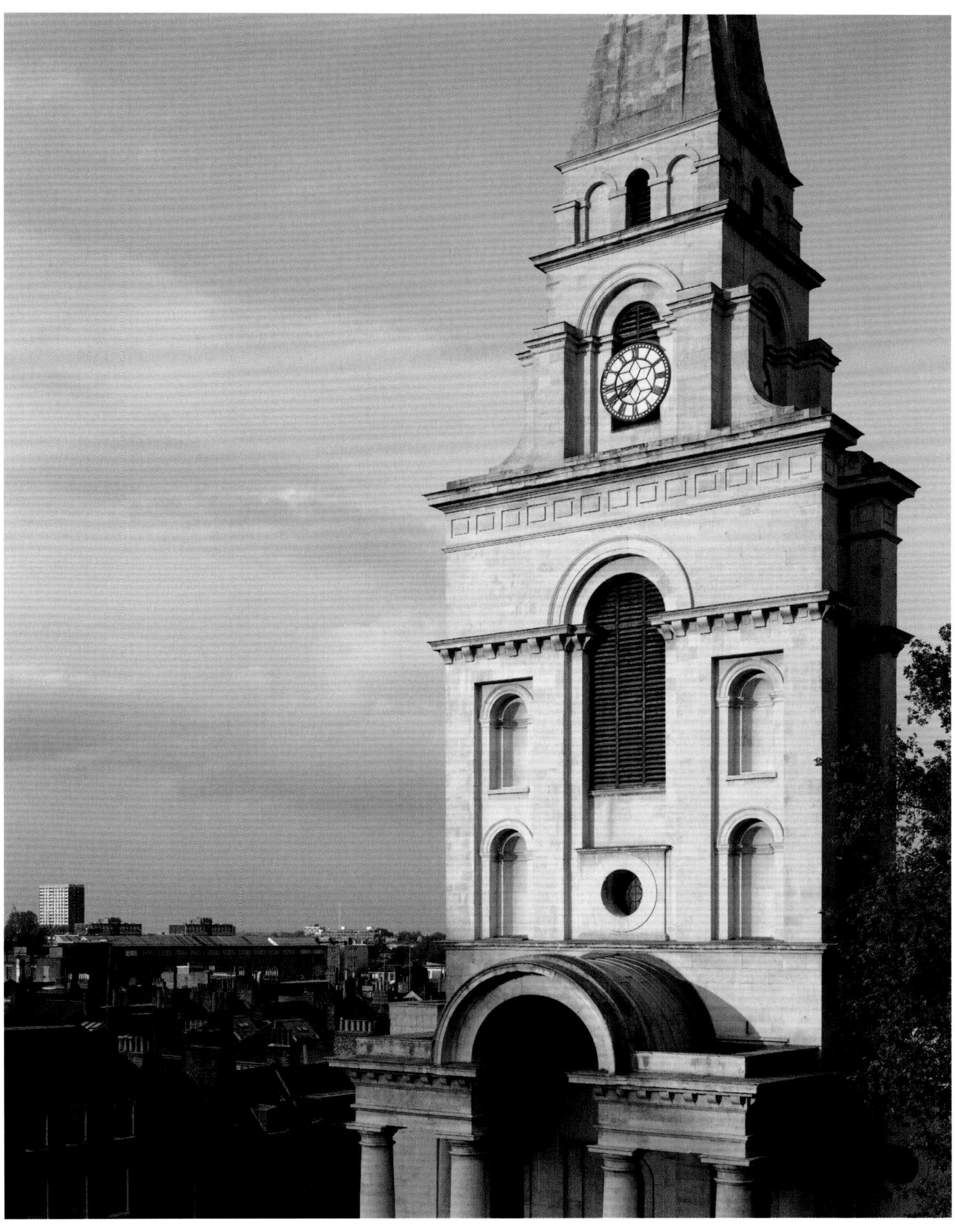

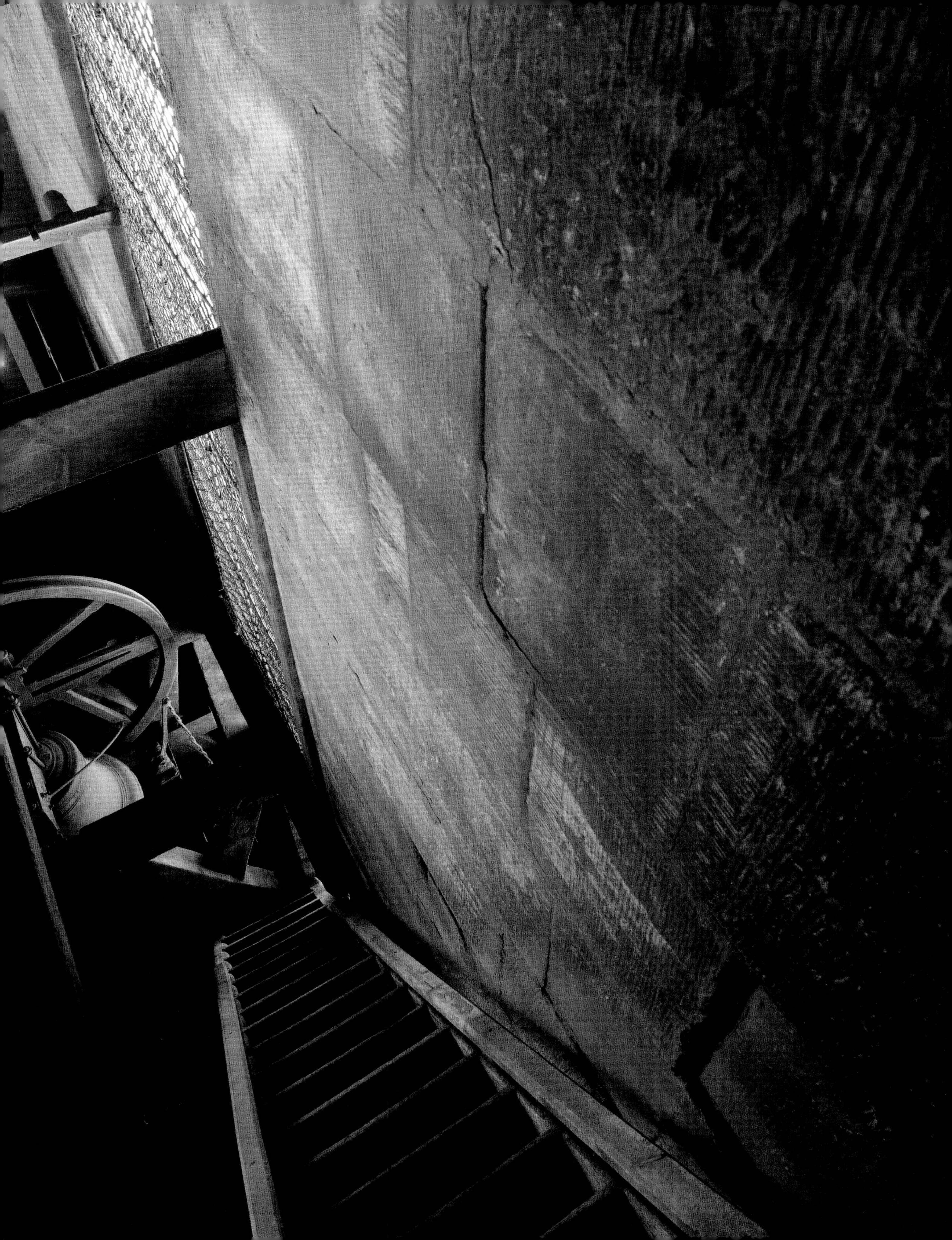

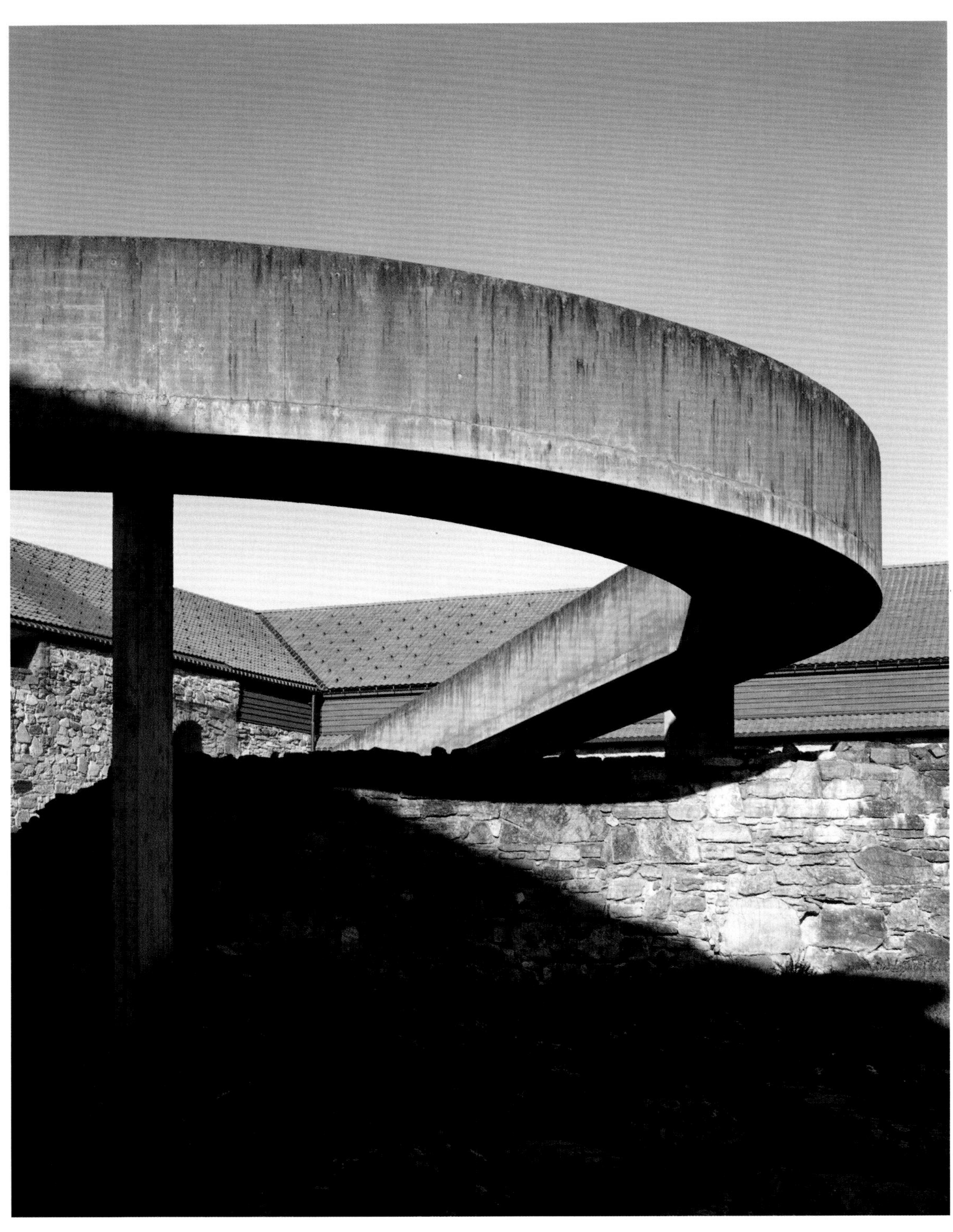

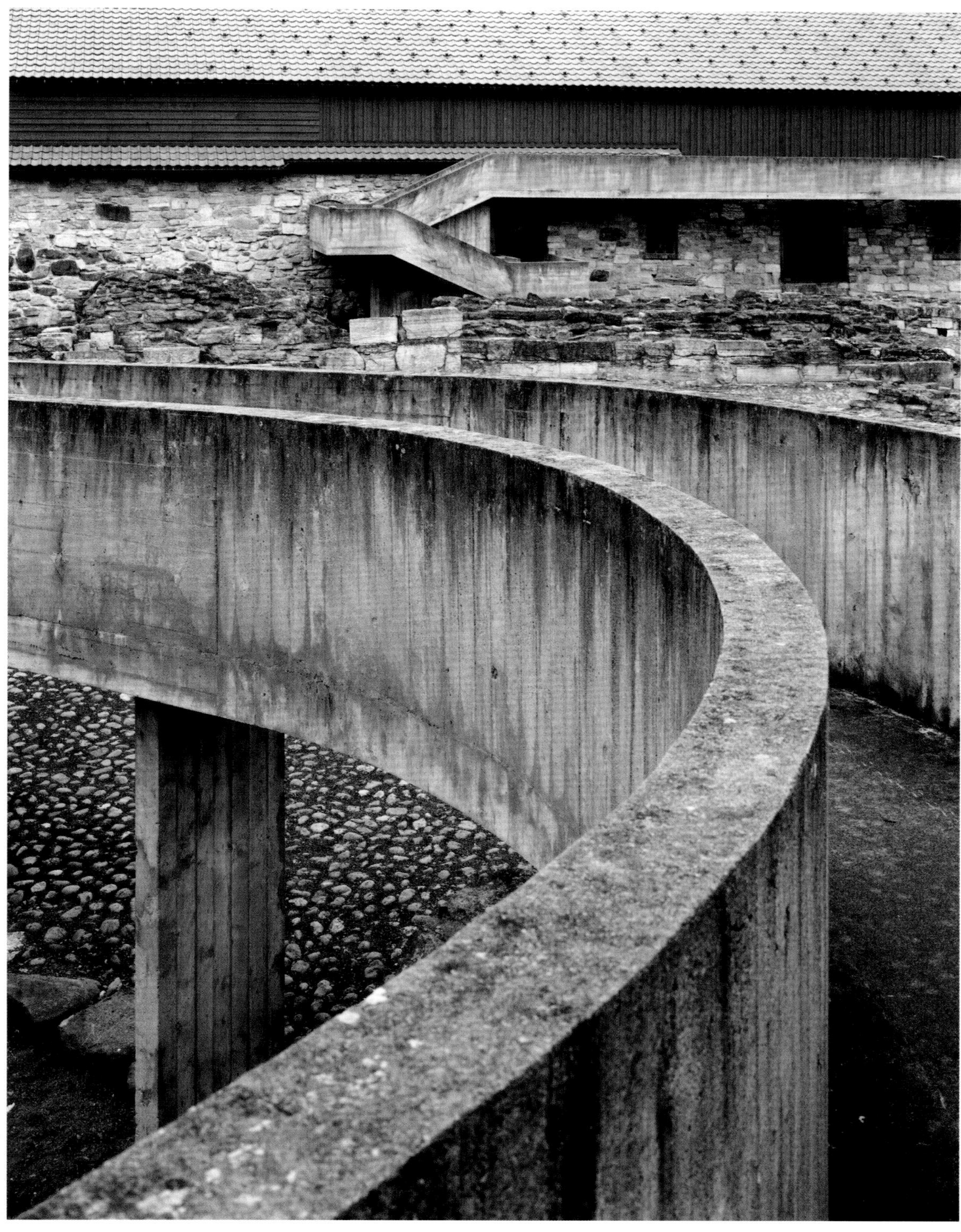

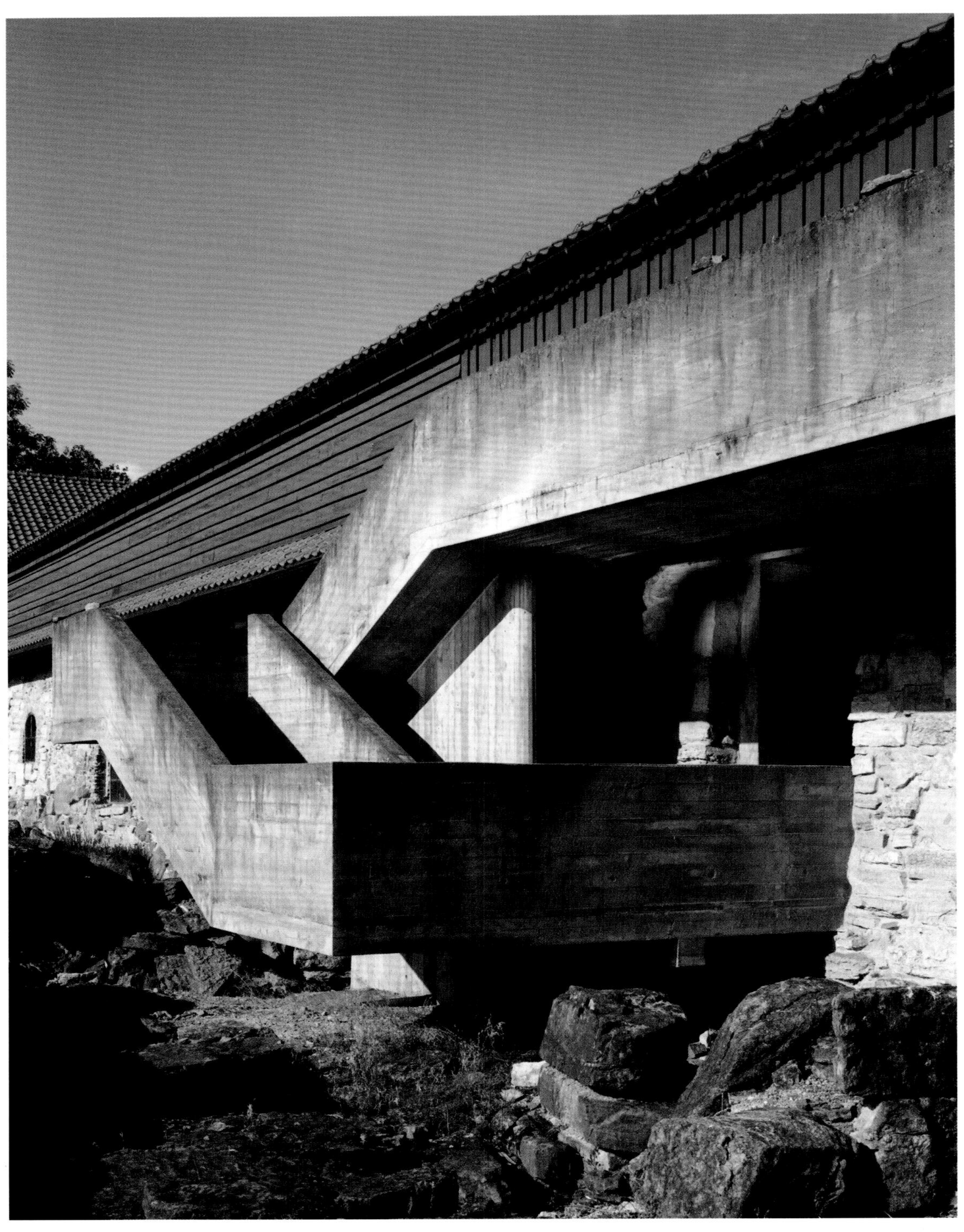

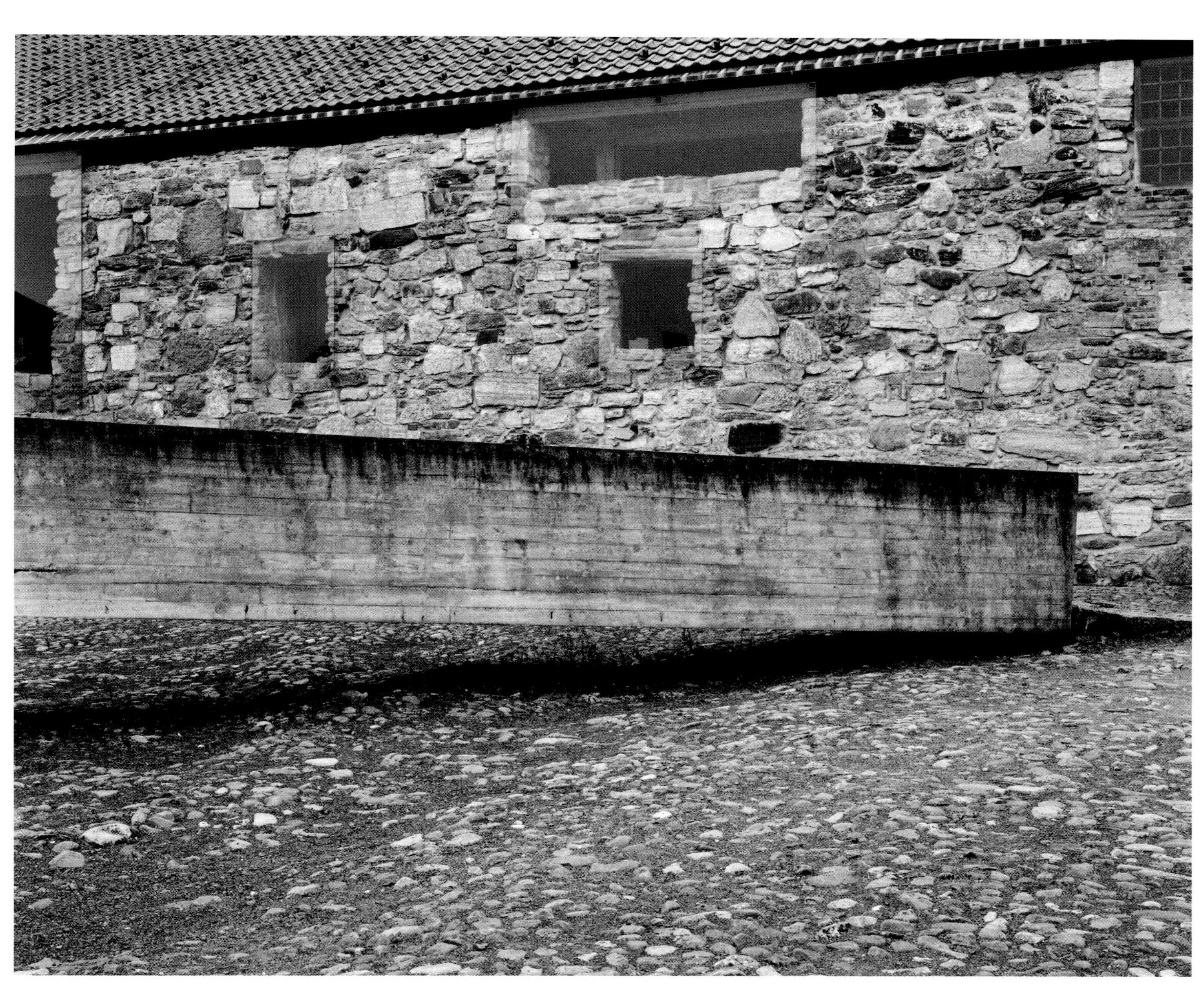

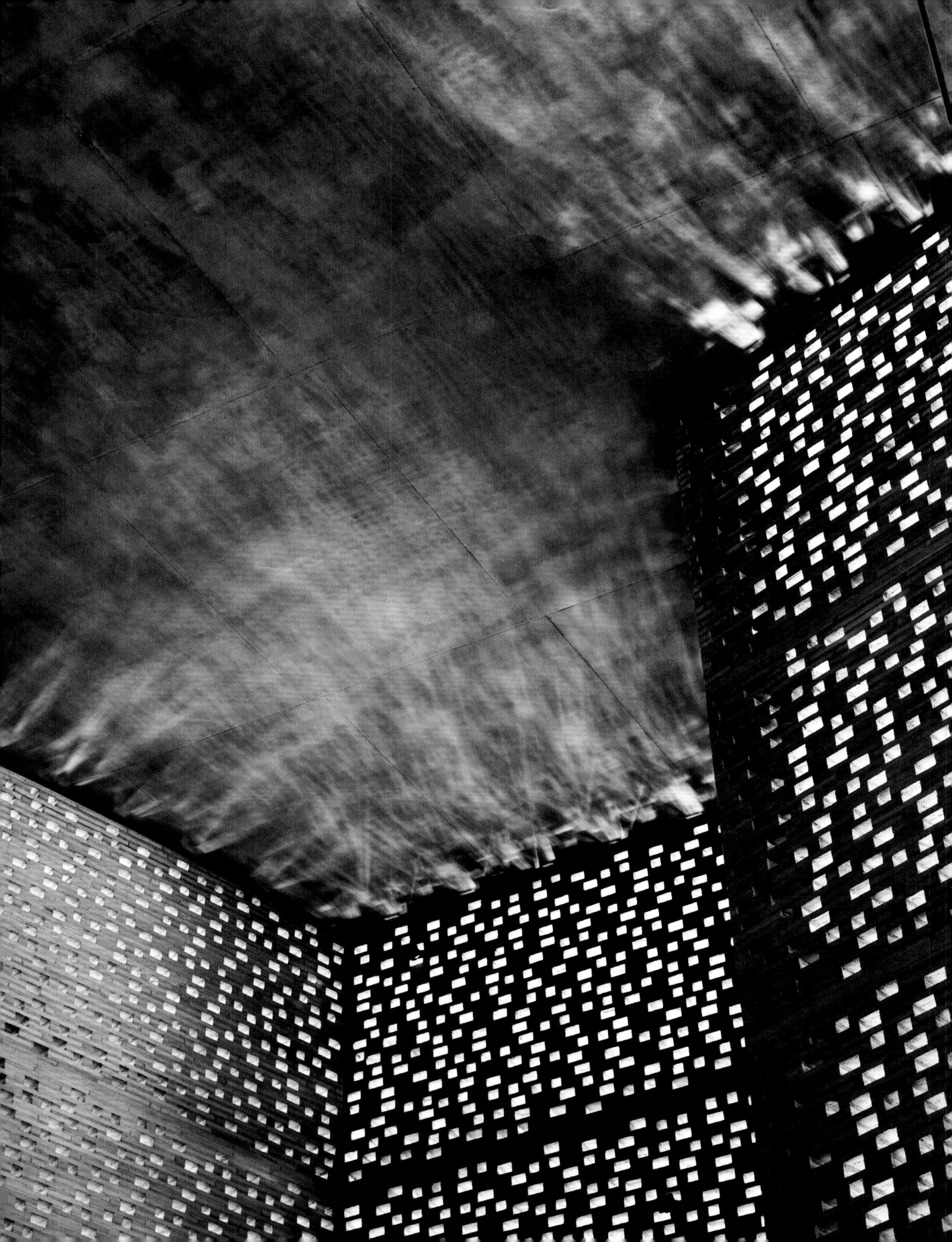

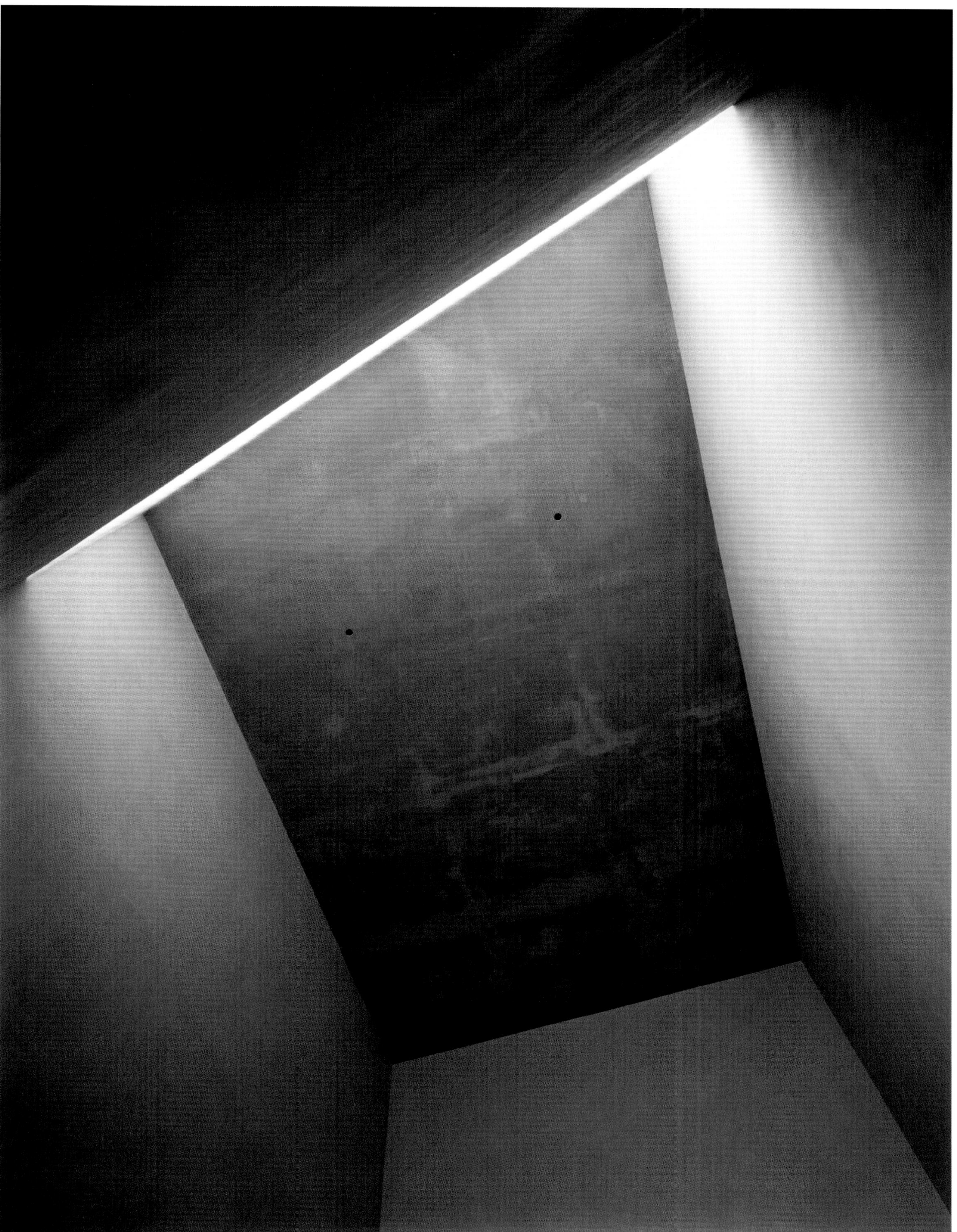

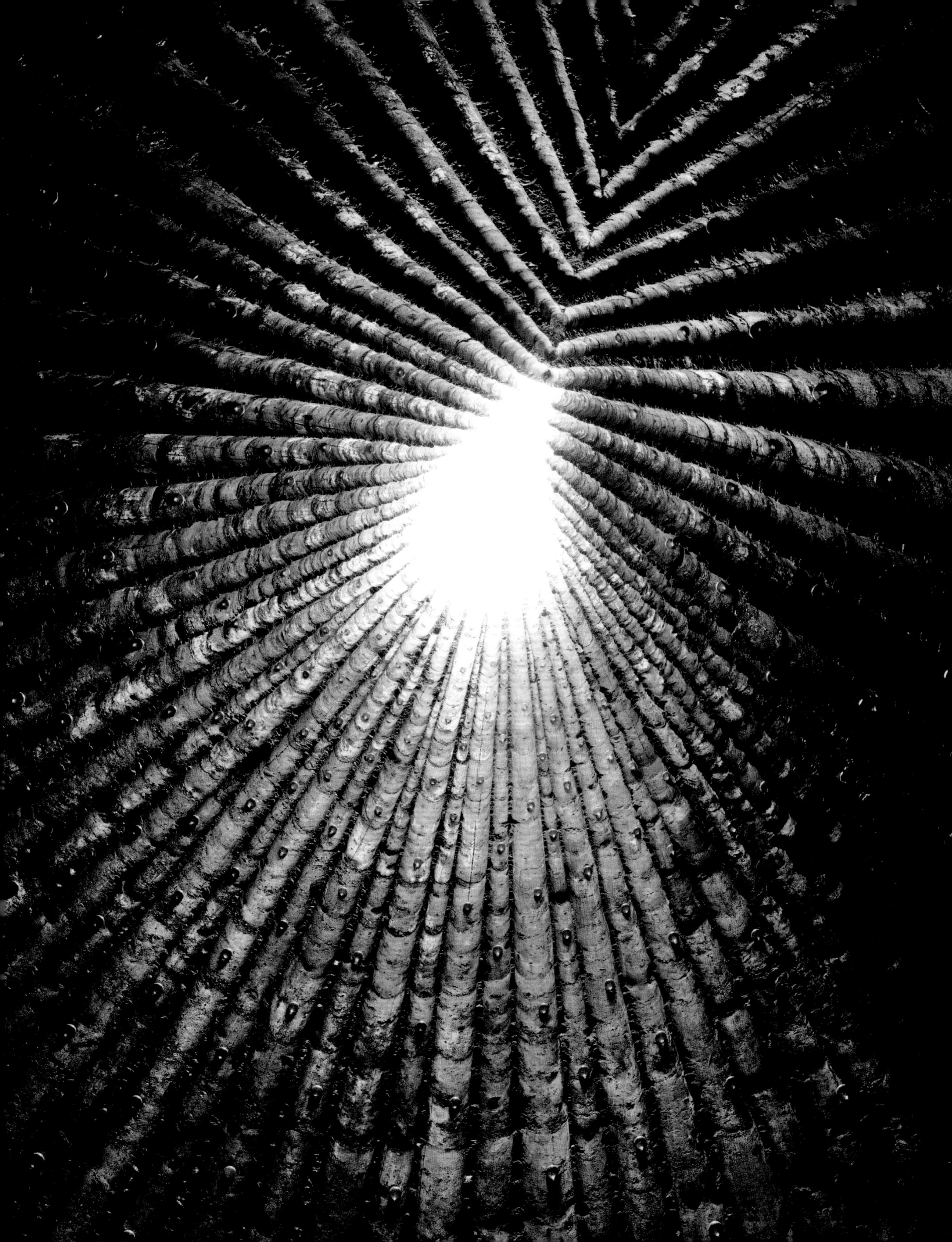

Plate Index

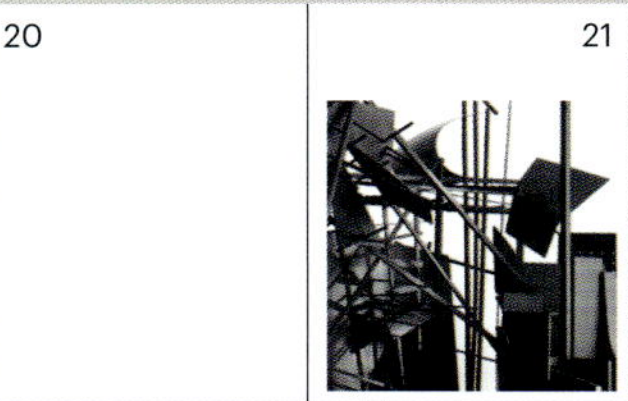 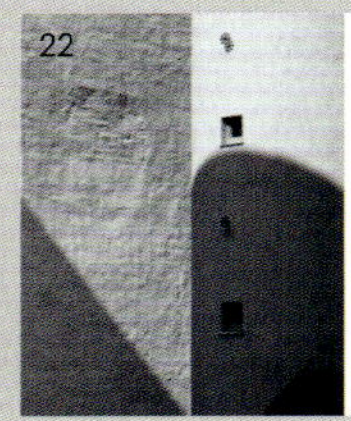 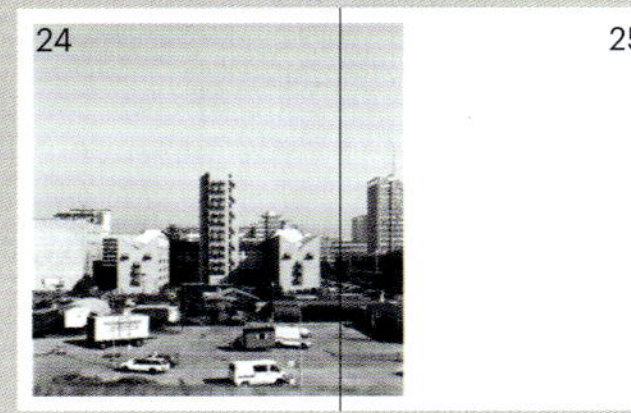 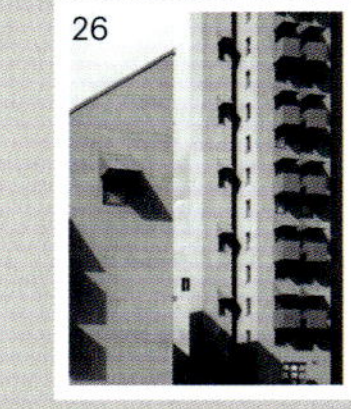 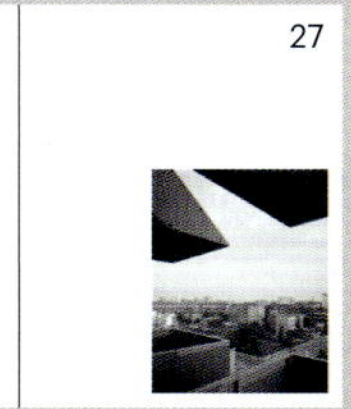

Daniel Libeskind / Studio Libeskind
House without Walls, 1986
Location: Milan, Italy
Completion: 1986
Hand-printed black-and-white
silver-gelatin print, 30×30 cm

John Hejduk
Kreuzberg Tower and Wings, 1988
Location: Berlin, Germany
Completion: 1988
Five hand-printed black-and-white
silver-gelatin prints, page 22: 36×29 cm;
pages 23–4: 30×30 cm; page 26:
37.5×26 cm; page 27: 36×29 cm

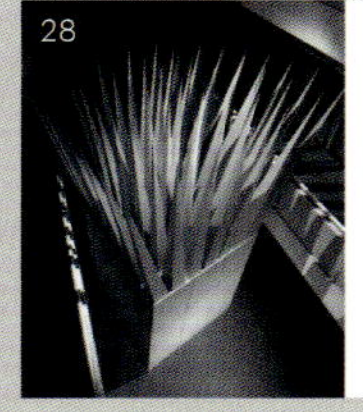 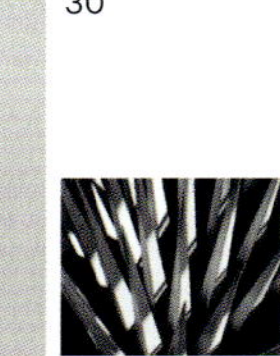 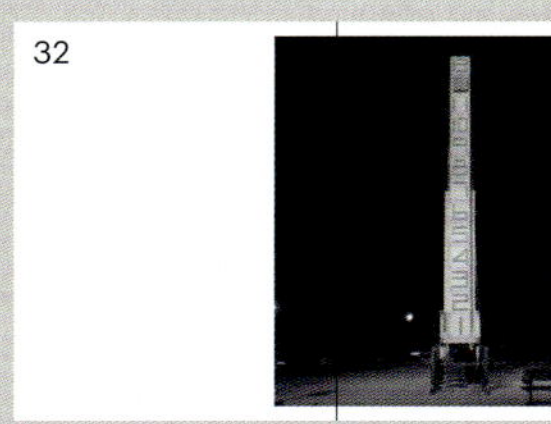 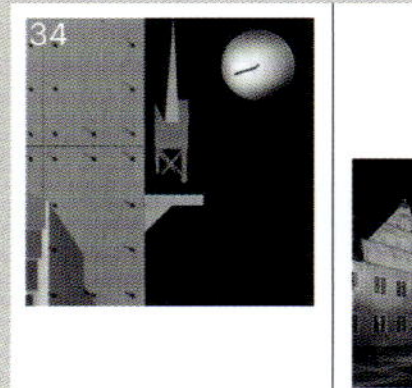

The House of the Suicide and The House
of the Mother of the Suicide, 1990
Location: Atlanta, United States
Completion: 1990
Three hand-printed black-and-white
silver-gelatin prints, page 28:
36×29 cm; page 29: 29×29 cm;
page 30: 29×36 cm

The House of the Suicide and The House
of the Mother of the Suicide, 1991
Location: Prague, Czech Republic
Completion: 1991
Hand-printed black-and-white
silver-gelatin print, page 31: 36×29 cm

The Collapse of Time, 1986
Location: London, United Kingdom
Completion: 1986
Hand-printed black-and-white
silver-gelatin print, 30×30 cm

Page 34: The Riga Project:
Object/Subject, 1987
Location: Philadelphia, United States
Completion: 1987
Page 35: Security, 1989
Location: Oslo, Norway
Completion: 1989
Two hand-printed black-and-white
silver-gelatin prints, page 34:
29×29 cm; page 35: 29×36 cm

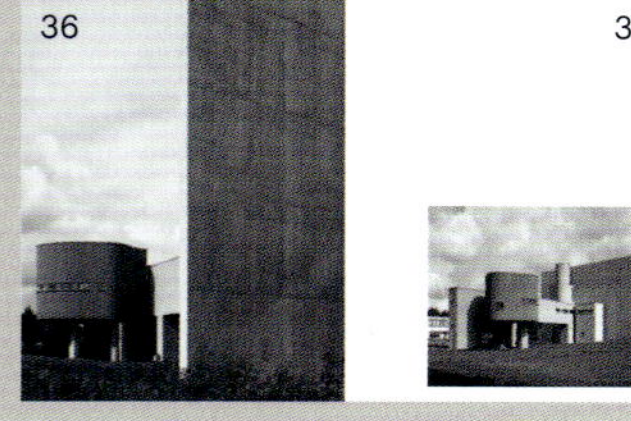 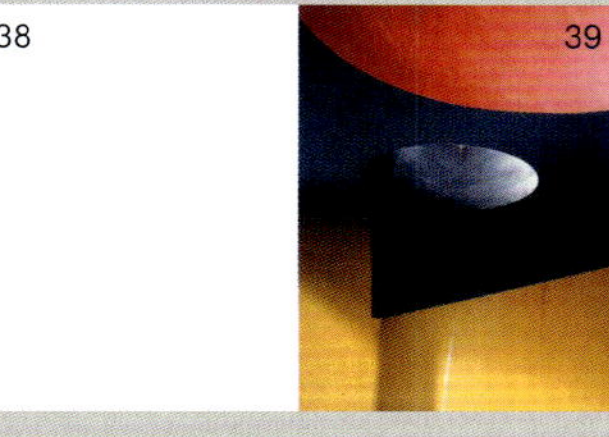 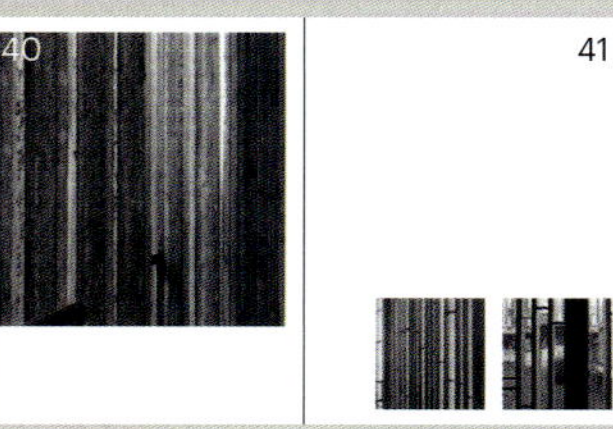 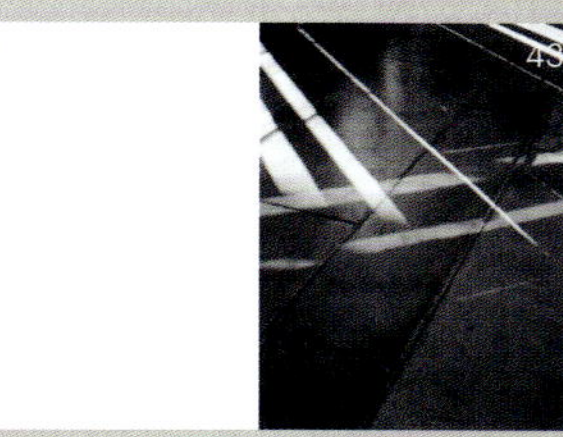

Wall House II, 2001
Location: Groningen, Netherlands
Completion: 2001
Two hand-printed black-and-white
silver-gelatin prints, page 36:
36×29 cm; page 37: 29×36 cm

Le Corbusier
'Canons de Lumière', Couvent
Sainte-Marie de la Tourette, 2007
Location: Eveux, France
Completion: 1961
Digital C-type print, 102×80 cm

Couvent Sainte-Marie de la Tourette, 2002
Location: Eveux, France
Completion: 1961
Ten hand-printed black-and-white
silver-gelatin prints, pages 40–1:
45×45 cm; pages 43–5: 100×80 cm;
pages 46–7: 39×39 cm

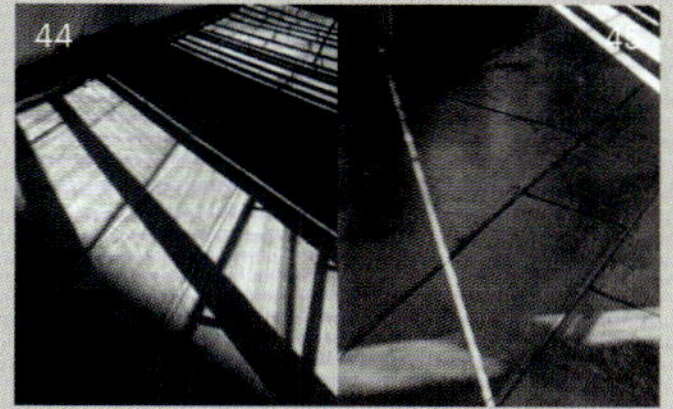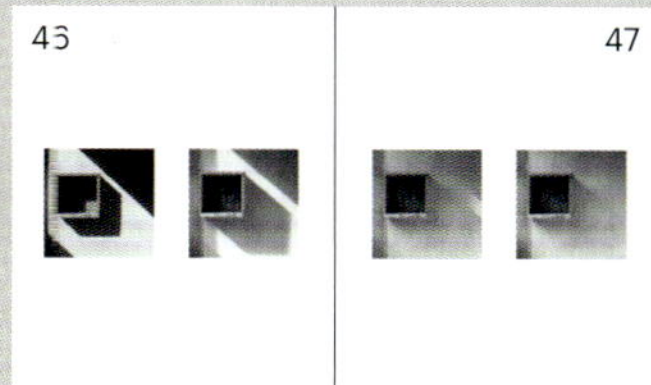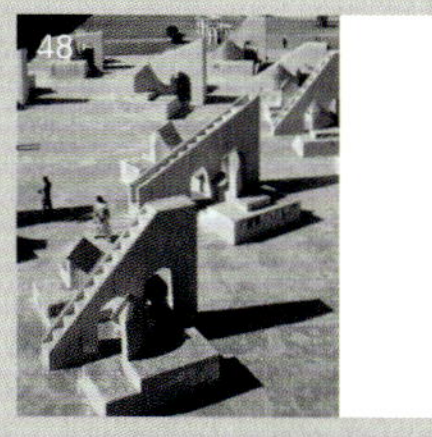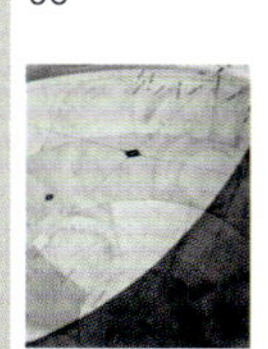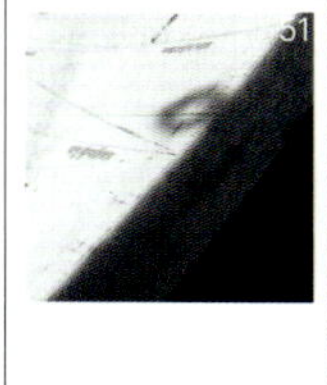

Jantar Mantar Observatory, 2002
Location: Jaipur, India
Completion: 1734
Three hand-printed black-and-white
silver-gelatin prints, pages 48,
50: 60×50 cm; page 51: 50×50 cm

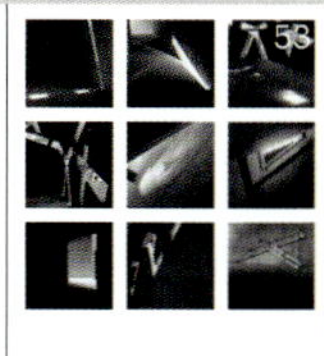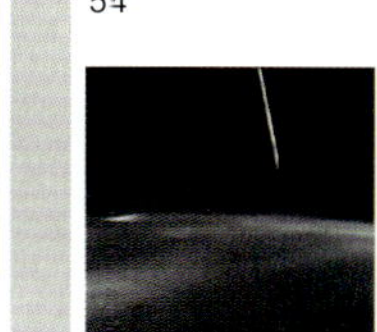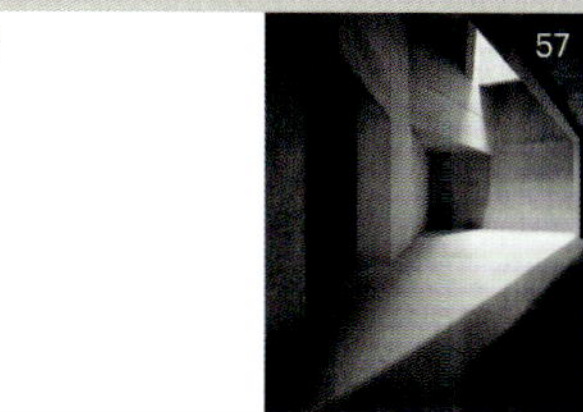

Daniel Libeskind / Studio Libeskind
Jewish Museum, 1996
Location: Berlin, Germany
Completion: 1999
Nine hand-printed black-and-white
silver-gelatin prints, 38.6×38.6 cm

Jewish Museum, 1996
Location: Berlin, Germany
Completion: 1999
Two digital black-and-white
silver-gelatin prints, page 54:
80×80 cm; page 57: 127×100 cm

Zaha Hadid Architects
Page 58: Landesgartenschau /
Landscape Formation One, 1999
Location: Weil am Rhein, Germany
Completion: 1999
Page 59: MAXXI – Museo nazionale delle
arti del XXI secolo, 2009
Location: Rome, Italy
Completion: 2010
Two digital black-and-white silver-gelatin
prints, page 58: 102×80 cm; page 59:
80×102 cm

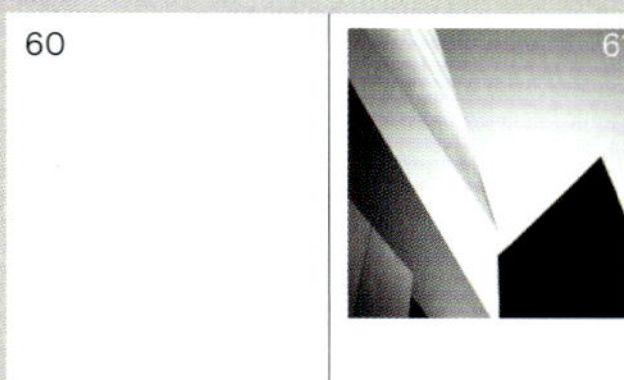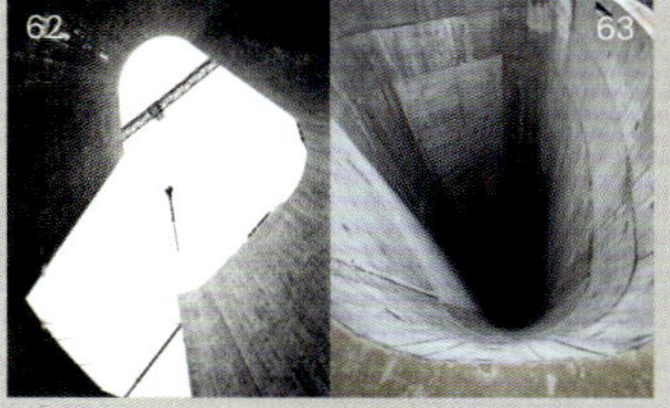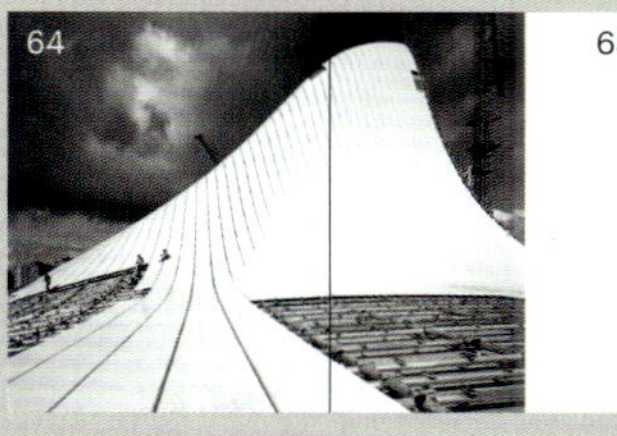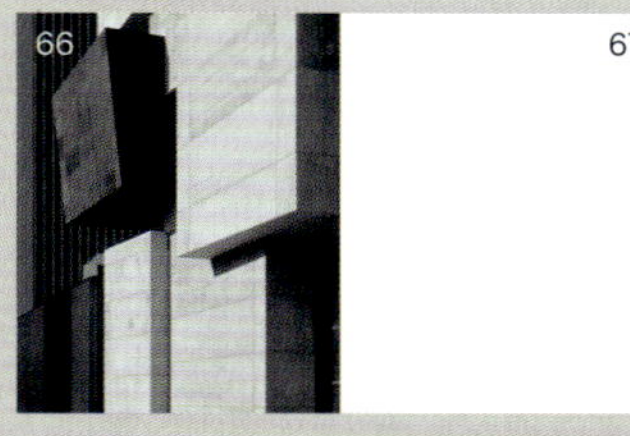

Vitra Fire Station, 1993
Location: Weil am Rhein, Germany
Completion: 1993
Digital black-and-white silver-gelatin
print, 80×80 cm

Phæno Science Center, page 62, 2003;
page 63, 2004
Location: Wolfsburg, Germany
Completion: 2005
Page 62: digital black-and-white
silver-gelatin print; page 63: digital
C-type print, both 102×80 cm

Heydar Aliyev Center, 2011
Location: Baku, Azerbaijan
Completion: 2012
Digital black-and-white silver-gelatin
print, 80×102 cm

Rosenthal Center for Contemporary
Art, 2003
Location: Cincinnati, United States
Completion: 2003
Digital black-and-white silver-gelatin
print, 127×100 cm

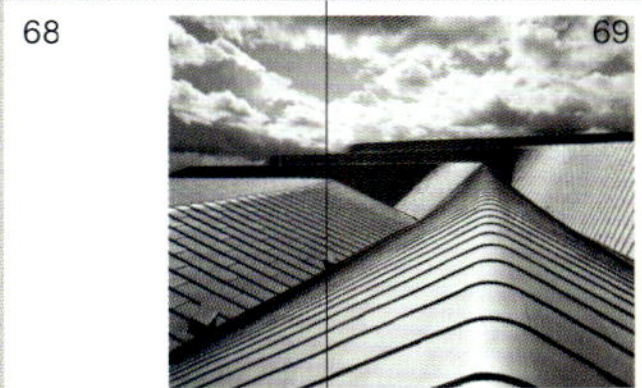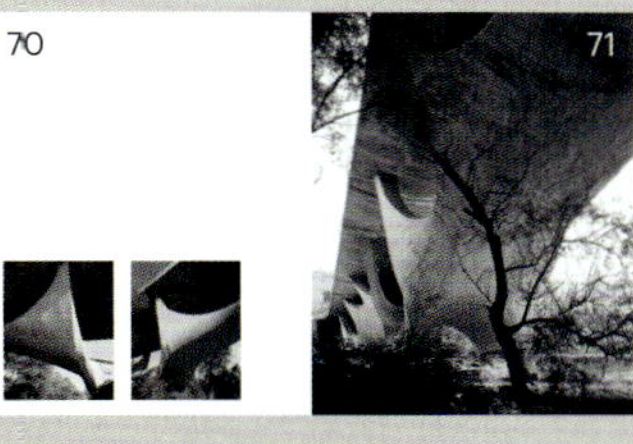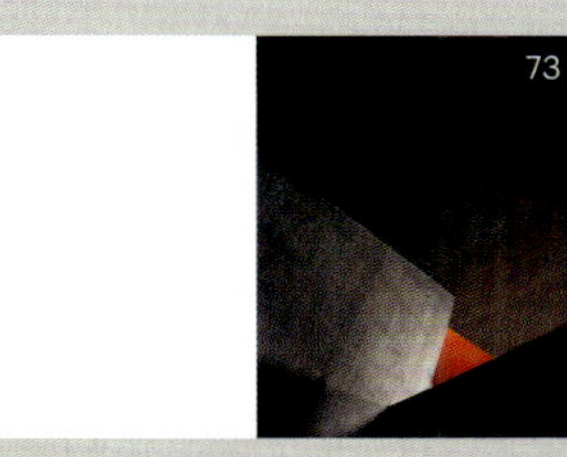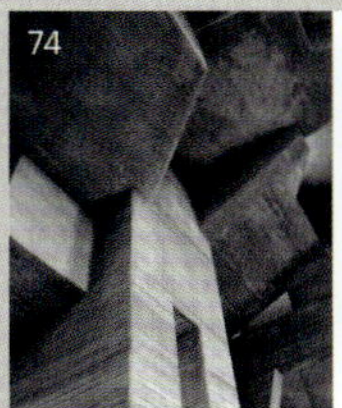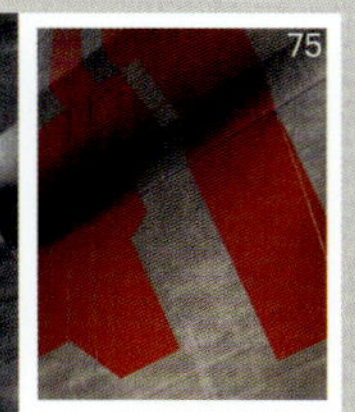

Riverside Museum, 2010
Location: Glasgow, United Kingdom
Completion: 2011
Digital black-and-white silver-gelatin
print, 80×102 cm

Sergio Musmeci
Ponte sul Basento, 2015
Location: Potenza, Italy
Completion: 1976
Three digital black-and-white
silver-gelatin prints, 153×120 cm

Gottfried Böhm
Church of St Matthew, 2020
Location: Düsseldorf, Germany
Completion: 1972
Digital C-type print, 102×80 cm

Page 74: Church of the Resurrection
of Christ, 2020
Location: Cologne, Germany
Completion: 1970
Digital black-and-white silver-gelatin
print, 102×80 cm
Page 75: Church of St Matthew, 2020
Location: Düsseldorf, Germany
Completion: 1972
Digital C-type print, 102×80 cm

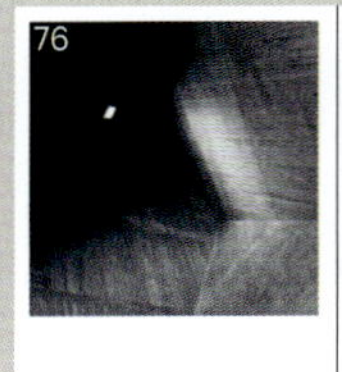

Church of St Gertrude, 2020
Location: Cologne, Germany
Completion: 1965
Five hand-printed black-and-white
silver-gelatin prints, 38.6×38.4 cm

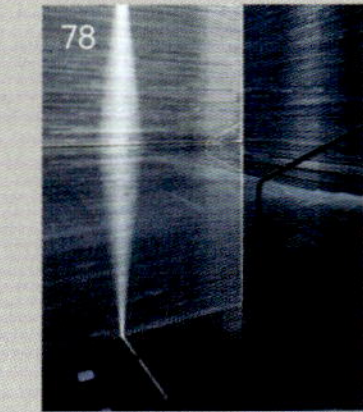

Atelier Peter Zumthor
Therme Vals, 2006
Location: Graubünden, Switzerland
Completion: 1996
Page 78: digital C-type print, 102×80 cm;
page 79: two digital black-and-white
silver-gelatin prints, 102×80 cm

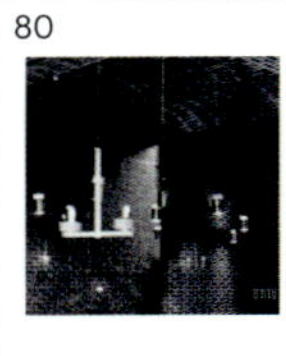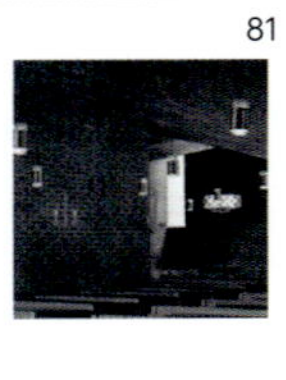

Sigurd Lewerentz
St Mark's Church, 1989
Location: Björkhagen, Stockholm, Sweden
Completion: 1960
Seven hand-printed black-and-white
silver-gelatin prints, 40×40 cm

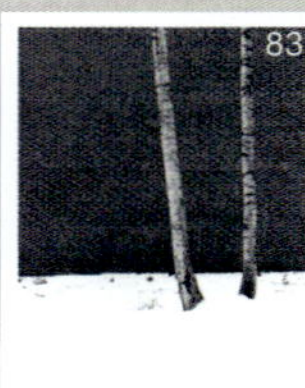

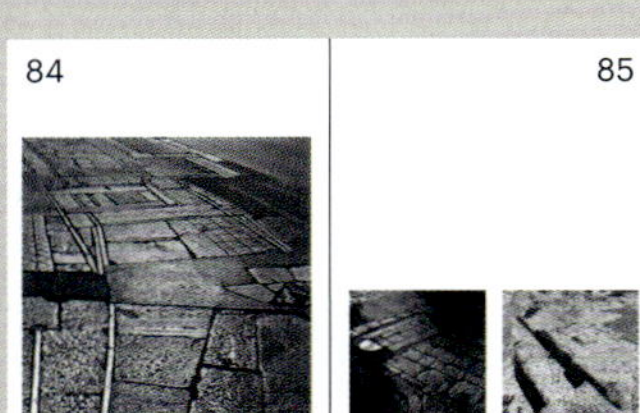

Dimitris Pikionis
Landscaping of the Acropolis, 1989
Location: Athens, Greece
Completion: 1957
Three digital black-and-white
silver-gelatin prints, 120×120 cm

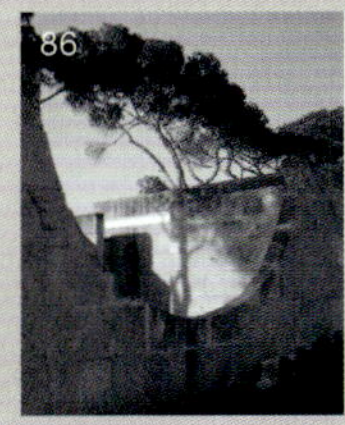

Jørn Utzon
Can Lis, 2019
Location: Mallorca, Spain
Completion: 1974
Two digital black-and-white
silver-gelatin prints, 102×80 cm

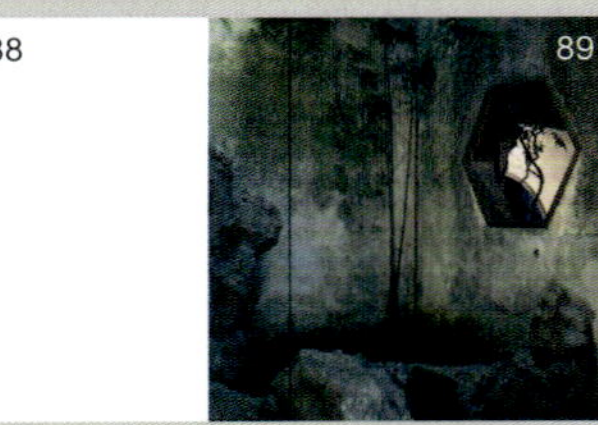

Classical Gardens of Suzhou
Lingering Garden, 2018
Location: Suzhou, China
Late sixteenth century (Ming Dynasty)
to twentieth century
Digital C-type print, 80×80 cm

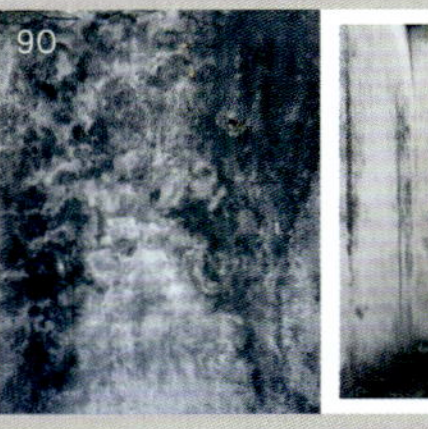

Humble Administrator's Garden, 2018
Location: Suzhou, China
Twelfth century (Southern Song Dynasty)
to twentieth century
Two digital C-type prints, 102×80 cm

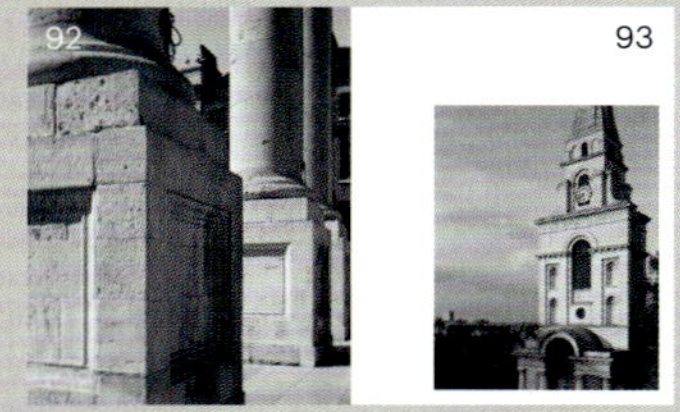

Nicholas Hawksmoor
Christ Church Spitalfields, 2012
Location: London, United Kingdom
Completion: 1729
Two digital black-and-white
silver-gelatin prints, 153×120 cm

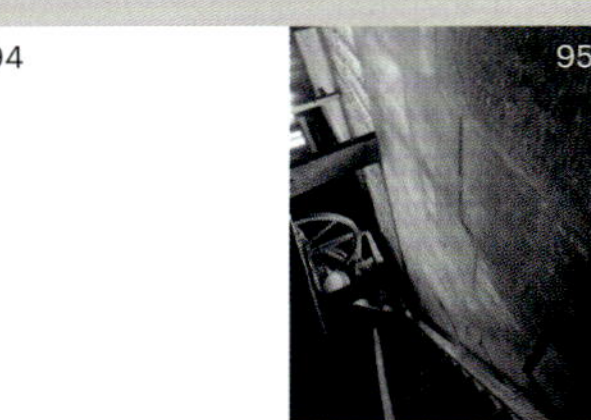

St Mary Woolnoth, 2012
Location: London, United Kingdom
Completion: 1724
Digital black-and-white
silver-gelatin print, 153×120 cm

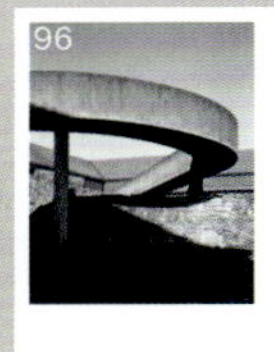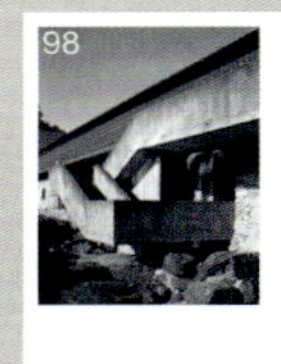

Sverre Fehn
Hedmark Museum, 2009
Location: Hamar, Norway
Completion: 1973
Four hand-printed black-and-white
silver-gelatin prints, pages 96–8:
58 4×46.9 cm; page 99: 46.9×58.4 cm

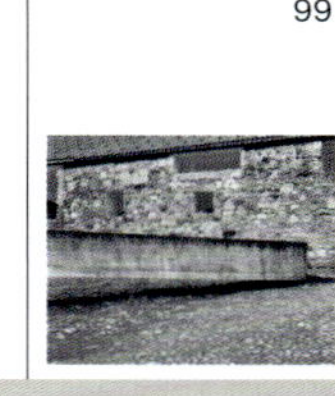

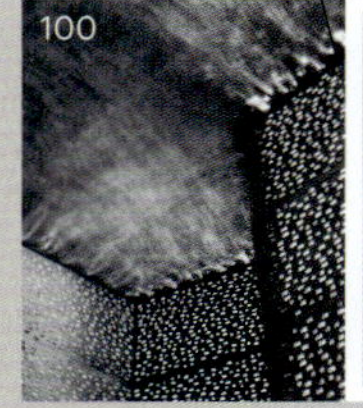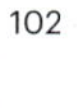

Atelier Peter Zumthor
Kolumba Museum, page 100, 2007;
page 101, 2008
Location: Cologne, Germany
Completion: 2007
Two digital black-and-white
silver-gelatin prints, 102×80 cm

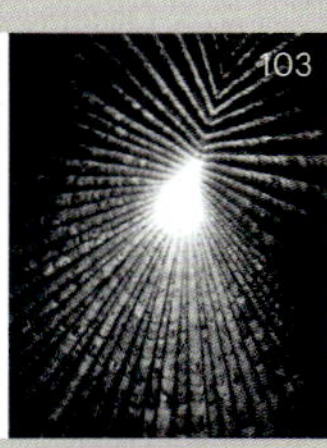

Bruder Klaus Field Chapel, 2009
Location: Wachendorf, Germany
Completion: 2007
Digital black-and-white silver-gelatin
print, 102×80 cm

The Architects and Their Buildings
Rhiannon Hope

John Hejduk (1929–2000)
The career of American architect, artist and educator John Hejduk spanned both modernist and post-modernist architectural thinking. His early work, which included **Wall House II** (designed in 1973 and completed posthumously in 2001), explored ideas of shape and spatial organisation in a manner reminiscent of Le Corbusier while his later practice foregrounded poetic and spiritual narratives.

Hejduk encouraged Binet to take up architectural photography, greatly influencing her approach: dissecting a building to explore its function and message and interrogating the nature of human experience within a built environment. One of Binet's earliest projects captured **The Collapse of Time** (1986), a temporary installation outside the Architectural Association in London that accompanied Hejduk's exhibition 'Victims' commemorating lives lost at the hands of the Gestapo in Berlin. Another temporary structure was **The House of the Suicide and The House of the Mother of the Suicide**, originally installed at the Georgia Institute of Technology, Atlanta, in 1990 and later rebuilt in Prague as a memorial to student Jan Palach, who died through self-immolation in protest at the 1968 Soviet invasion of Czechoslovakia. Hejduk also designed a series of projects known as 'masques' that explored the narrative potential of architecture, including **The Riga Project: Object/Subject** (1987) and **Security** (1989). A rare permanent building was the fourteen-storey **Kreuzberg Tower and Wings** (1988) commissioned as part of the International BauAufstellung (IBA) programme to build low-income housing in West Berlin.

Le Corbusier (1887–1965)
Swiss architect Charles-Edouard Jeanneret, better known as Le Corbusier, was one of the most important and controversial architects and urban planners of the twentieth century. Binet was introduced to his work by Jean Petit (1927–1999), who designed many of Le Corbusier's early publications. The **Couvent Sainte-Marie de la Tourette** (1961) near Lyon, created in collaboration with Iannis Xenakis (1922–2001) and one of Le Corbusier's last completed buildings in Europe, is a demonstration of his key architectural principles, with its dynamic, raw-concrete façade, pilotis, grass-covered roof and horizontal bands of glazing. Light entering the chapel from a single square opening in the roof and two strips of six rectangles along the side walls is channelled via a system of prisms into the sacristy and crypt below, spotlighting the bold red, yellow and blue walls. The simplicity of the chapel interior expresses the spiritual nature of a space designed for silent devotion.

Jantar Mantar Observatory
Built during the construction of the city of Jaipur as commanded by the ruler Jai Singh II, the **Jantar Mantar Observatory** (1734) is a monumental series of nineteen astronomical structures. Each was designed to enable precise observations that could be used to predict the movements of the sun, moon and planets, act as a world clock, and even estimate the arrival of the monsoon season – all based on the principles of Ptolemaic astronomy. Le Corbusier visited the site and was inspired by the Jantar Mantar not only as a space where light and darkness were used to understand the cosmos but also for the scale of humanity's attempt to comprehend its surroundings. Binet made the same pilgrimage as research for her photographic essay on the Couvent Sainte-Marie de la Tourette for the exhibition she co-curated, 'The Secret of the Shadow: Light and Shadow in Architecture', at the Deutsches Architekturmuseum in Frankfurt in 2002.

Daniel Libeskind Hon RA (b. 1946)
Polish-American architect Daniel Libeskind originally had ambitions to become a professional musician. After anti-semitism forced his family to leave Poland and emigrate to the United States he turned to architecture, attending The Cooper Union in New York, where John Hejduk was one of his tutors. Like Hejduk and Hadid, Libeskind was initially known for his 'paper architecture', exploring ideas through drawing, writing and installations. One of Binet's first encounters with his dynamic practice was **House without Walls** (1986), exhibited at the Milan Triennale. In 1989 he won the competition to design the **Jewish Museum** (1999) in Berlin, a building whose violent geometries, acute angles and seemingly impenetrable voids force an encounter with absence and the horrors of the Holocaust. The first of her projects to capture a space so bound up with meaning, Binet's work on the Jewish Museum played a fundamental role in her development as a photographer.

Zaha Hadid RA (1950–2016)
The British-Iraqi architect Zaha Hadid reinvented the idea of expressionism in building for the latter part of the twentieth century and in 2004 became the first woman to be awarded the Pritzker Prize. She established her own practice in 1977, but despite acclaim for her drawings and paintings and her inclusion in the 1988 exhibition 'Deconstructivist Architecture' at MoMA in New York she built little until the **Vitra Fire Station** (1993) at Weil am Rhein, where the characteristic intersecting planes and sharp linearity reflect the building's function.

Hadid commissioned many photographers, wanting her buildings to be appreciated from multiple perspectives. Granting Binet a great deal of latitude and freeing her from the need to capture a building in its entirety enabled her to produce photographs that become abstract studies of light and form, conveying unexpected perspectives and exploring stark contrasts in her images of **Landesgartenschau / Landscape Formation One** (1999), also at Weil am Rhein, and the **Rosenthal Center for Contemporary Art** (2003) in Cincinnati. The intersecting volumes of the **MAXXI** (2010) in Rome are brought into sharp focus through the calculated use of natural light while at the **Riverside Museum** (2011) in Glasgow Binet captures the sinuous curves that became synonymous with Hadid's later work. By recording buildings still under construction, including the **Phæno Science Center** (2005) in Wolfsburg and the **Heydar Aliyev Center** (2012) in Baku, Binet's work emphasises the power of making and the strength inherent in the materials employed, particularly concrete.

Sergio Musmeci (1926–1981)
An Italian civil engineer famed for his model-based experimentation into the stresses within architectural structures, Sergio Musmeci designed the **Ponte sul Basento** (1976) to connect southern and central Potenza in southern Italy. Developed before the era of computer-aided design, its curved elements were constructed with the help of a boat-builder from Naples who created wooden moulds for the dramatically contorted arches. Made from a reinforced-concrete membrane only about 30 centimetres thick, the daring structure was greatly admired by many architects, including Zaha Hadid. Binet views Musmeci's design

as a celebration of the expressive possibilities of concrete and this exhibition is the first time images of projects by Hadid and Musmeci have been brought together, a personal wish of the former.

Gottfried Böhm (1920–2021)
The first German architect to be awarded the Pritzker Prize, Gottfried Böhm is known for highly sculptural concrete buildings including a remarkable series of churches. Under the guidance of his architect father Dominikus Böhm (1880–1955), whose practice he led from 1955, Böhm developed a style of drawing that translated directly into the structures and surfaces of his work.

Commissioned by the Museum Angewandte Kunst in Cologne to celebrate the centenary of Böhm's birth, Binet's photographs explore his vision for spiritual architecture in Germany. Complex cuboid volumes are foregrounded in both the **Church of the Resurrection of Christ** (1970) in Cologne and the **Church of St Matthew** (1972) in Düsseldorf. In the latter, these volumes are set between rounded towers and exposed concrete positioned next to painted brickwork to create a series of complex interconnecting spaces and surfaces. A faceted concrete roof soars above the altar while the halls leading off the central space allow changing rays of light to penetrate the building, creating a sense of intimacy. In the **Church of St Gertrude** (1965) in Cologne, Böhm takes the approach even further, using folds of concrete that integrate ceiling and wall to create a continuous modelled volume. Outside, the height of the ancillary buildings matches that of the street line while the expressive architectural language of the soaring tower and the church itself distinguish its spiritual project from its neighbours.

Sigurd Lewerentz (1885–1975)
One of the leading Swedish architects of the twentieth century, Sigurd Lewerentz created structures that question what it is to be human, to experience space, light and life. His long career began in partnership with Gunnar Asplund (1885–1940) on the design of the Woodland Cemetery in Stockholm, moving into a period focused on functional design and the production of industrial components before returning to his probing, transcendent approach at **St Mark's Church** (1960), also in Stockholm. Here Lewerentz's expressive use of brick is made even more powerful through a restrained treatment of windows,

with large expanses of wall punctuated only by the shadows cast by trees in the surrounding parkland. Inside, vaulted brick ceilings meet simple brick walls, the visual effect articulated through shifting volumes and hanging light fittings that in Binet's photographs seem suspended in both space and time.

Dimitris Pikionis (1887–1968)
Greek architect and artist Dimitris Pikionis combined an academic background in civil engineering with a love of painting refined during studies in Paris and Munich. After returning to Greece, he designed a series of modernist projects that were nevertheless imbued with a sense of place. Considered his greatest achievement, **Landscaping of the Acropolis** (1957) celebrates the physical history of the region through a series of pedestrian pathways leading to the ancient citadel. Local stone, fragments from antiquity and rubble salvaged from nineteenth-century houses demolished during the expansion of Athens are positioned in apparently irregular but geometrically patterned trails. Binet's work foregrounds these pathways, revealing the rich materiality of the individual stones and allowing us to view the work as a singular piece of landscape.

Jørn Utzon (1918–2008)
Danish architect Jørn Utzon is celebrated for his success in the 1955 Sydney Opera House competition, a project he abandoned a decade later because of political disputes affecting the design. Already well-travelled, with time spent in Sweden, Japan, India, Mexico and the United States, he decided to settle with his family in Mallorca. There he designed **Can Lis** (1974), a villa overlooking the sea, developing his distinctive approach to space and proportion and working closely with a local builder to use traditional methods and materials. Binet's photographs avoid the Greek-temple imagery often found in pictures of Can Lis, instead capturing a feeling inextricably linked to Utzon's reflections on space, perception of nature and ways of working with the landscape.

Classical Gardens of Suzhou
The development of the Classical Gardens of Suzhou, a UNESCO World Heritage site, spans several dynasties and nearly a thousand years, from the twelfth century. Binet's compositions focus on the walls of the **Humble Administrator's Garden** and the **Lingering Garden**, exploring the possibility of architecture transforming into landscape. The wall is seen as a living surface that grows and evolves over time, with physical and spiritual history bound up in the skin of the structure. One of Binet's recent projects, commissioned for a solo exhibition in Shanghai, this series marks a move away from the interrogation of ideas of space in architecture, instead evoking a dreamlike, mythological quality where architecture becomes a frame for imagined landscapes suffused with experience, memory and a sense of place.

Nicholas Hawksmoor (c. 1661–1736)
A master of English Baroque, Nicholas Hawksmoor worked first as an assistant to Sir Christopher Wren (1632–1723). By 1711, when the Commission for Building Fifty New Churches was established to provide places of worship for the expanding populations on the outskirts of London, he had already stepped out of Wren's shadow and was working on large-scale projects with Sir John Vanbrugh (1664–1726). Of the twelve Commission churches completed, six were designed by Hawksmoor in his idiosyncratically sculptural style: never having left England, his understanding of Greek and Roman architecture was derived from literature and drawings. His imaginative translations of classical proportions and principles can be seen in **Christ Church Spitalfields** (1729), where a Roman-inspired columned portico is combined with an English gothic steeple and surprising details in window groupings and shadow patterns. Hawksmoor's distinctive approach continues at the City church of **St Mary Woolnoth** (1724), where imposing Tuscan columns are scored to match the rustication of the façade and twin turrets perch above a Composite order.

Sverre Fehn (1924–2009)
Norwegian architect Sverre Fehn trained with Jean Prouvé (1901–1984) before becoming a member of the progressive movement in post-war Scandinavian architecture. One of his most significant projects, the **Hedmark Museum** (1973) in Hamar, has a rich history embedded within its foundations. The focus of this regional museum was the display of excavated objects found in the area, recording and preserving the history of the land and its people. Fehn's task was to create a new structure integrating the ruins of an early nineteenth-century barn and traces of

a medieval fortress. Principles absorbed during his time with Prouvé and from later studies of Moroccan architecture, combined with his understanding of materials and the need to respond to location, are visible throughout. Binet's compositions foreground the sweeping concrete ramps that lead visitors into the museum, piercing ancient stone walls and timber frames salvaged from the historic structures and offering views down to the excavated foundations of earlier buildings on the site.

Peter Zumthor Hon RA (b. 1943)

Swiss architect Peter Zumthor's buildings achieve a symbiosis with the landscape, responding to local, natural and material concerns in a way that is evoked in Binet's equally experiential compositions. His manipulation of light can be seen in the delicately perforated brickwork of the **Kolumba Museum** (2007) in Cologne and in the design of **Therme Vals** (1996), a sequence of buildings subsumed into the landscape and harnessing natural springs. Here Zumthor crafts arresting views throughout the internal spaces, using natural light and the thermal waters as his materials alongside concrete and local quartz stone. The **Bruder Klaus Field Chapel** (2007) in Wachendorf is striking in its form and its unusual method of construction: 112 tree trunks were tightly bound in a tapering frame over which concrete was poured. The timber structure was then burnt away, leaving a negative space, a charred cavity that contrasts with the smooth exterior walls. The ruggedness of the internal surfaces is emphasised by light pouring through an open oculus, connecting spirituality with the natural world. The interior of the chapel remains exposed to the elements, so changing weather and the passage of time constantly modify the monastic, intimate atmosphere within.

Biography

Hélène Binet (b. 1959) is an internationally acclaimed photographer based in London but originally from Sorengo, Switzerland. She studied photography at the Istituto Europeo di Design in Rome, the city in which she spent most of her formative years. Over a period of more than 35 years Binet has captured both contemporary and historic architecture. She is a fervent advocate of analogue photography, working exclusively with film, and a firm believer that 'the soul of photography is its relationship with the instant'.

Binet's work has been exhibited in both national and international exhibitions, including a solo exhibition at the Power Station of Art, Shanghai, in 2019. She was made an Honorary Fellow of the Royal Institute of British Architects in 2007 and in 2015 was the recipient of the Julius Shulman Institute Excellence in Photography Award. She was also the recipient of the 2019 Ada Louise Huxtable Prize, awarded to a woman who has made a major contribution to architecture, and is one of the Royal Photographic Society's Hundred Heroines.

Selected Publications

Hélène Binet, *The Intimacy of Making: Three Historical Sites in Korea*, Zürich, 2021

Hélène Binet, *The Walls of Suzhou Gardens: A Photographic Journey*, Zürich, 2021

Kashef Chowdhury, *The Friendship Centre: Gaibandha, Bangladesh*, Zürich, 2016

Mohsen Mostafavi and Hélène Binet, *Nicholas Hawksmoor: London Churches*, Zürich, 2015

Hélène Binet, *Composing Space: The Photographs of Hélène Binet*, London and New York, 2012

Raoul Bunschoten and Hélène Binet, *A Passage Through Silence and Light: Daniel Libeskind's Extension to the Berlin Museum*, London, 2001

Peter Zumthor and Hélène Binet, *Peter Zumthor Works: Buildings and Projects, 1979–1997*, Basel, 1999

Supporters of the Royal Academy of Arts

The President's Circle
Blavatnik Family Foundation
The Clore Duffield Foundation
Mervyn and Jeanne Davies
The Dorfman Foundation
Dunard Fund
Mrs Drue Heinz Hon DBE
National Lottery Heritage Fund
Mrs Gabrielle Jungels-Winkler
Ronald and Rita McAulay
The McLennan Family
Sir John Madejski OBE DL
The Mead Family Foundation
Mr and Mrs Robert Miller
The Monument Trust
Julia and Hans Rausing
Simon and Virginia Robertson
The Rothschild Foundation
Dame Jillian Sackler DBE
The Garfield Weston Foundation
The Maurice Wohl Charitable
  Foundation
The Wolfson Foundation

**Major benefactors of the
redevelopment project**
The Band Trust
The 29th May 1961 Charitable
  Trust
Ambassador Matthew Barzun and
  Brooke Brown Barzun
Aryeh and Elana Bourkoff,
  LionTree
Sir Francis and the Hon Lady
  Brooke
The Cadogan Charity
Sir Richard and Lady Carew Pole
Chenevière Travel Award
Adrian Cheng
Jeremy Coller Foundation
John and Gail Coombe
Sir Roger de Grey Memorial Fund
Lady Alison Deighton
The Eranda Rothschild Foundation
Peter Greenham Fund
The Fidelity UK Foundation
The Foyle Foundation
J Paul Getty Jr Charitable Trust
Horace W Goldsmith Foundation
Mr and Mrs Jim Grover
The Alexis and Anne-Marie Habib
  Foundation
Charles and Kaaren Hale
E Vincent Harris Fund
Nicolette and Frederick Kwok
The Kirby Laing Foundation
Lord Leverhulme's Charitable
  Trust
Christian Levett and Mougins
  Museum of Classical Art
The Linbury Trust
Miss Rosemary Lomax Simpson
Mr William Loschert
Molly Lowell and David Borthwick
  Maintenance Fund
Philip and Valerie Marsden
The Lord Mayor's Appeal
The Paul Mellon Estate
Milner Educational Trust
The Batia and Idan Ofer Family
  Foundation
Christina Ong
The Estate of the late Miss
  Constance-Anne Parker
J Heritage Peters
P F Charitable Trust
John Porter Charitable Trust
The Porter Foundation
Schools Portfolio Fund
Ivor Rey Scholarship Fund
The Schroder Foundation
Mr Sean Scully RA

Jake and Hélène Marie Shafran
Mr Richard S Sharp
William and Maureen Shenkman
Dasha Shenkman
The Estate of the late Mrs Pauline
  Sitwell
Starr Fund
David and Deborah Stileman
The Swire Charitable Trust
The late Sir Anthony Tennant and
  Lady Tennant
The Thompson Family Charitable
  Trust
Patricia Turner Award
Vandaleur
Sir Siegmund Warburg's Voluntary
  Settlement
The Welton Foundation
Mr W Galen Weston and the Hon
  Mrs Hilary Weston

**Benefactors of the
redevelopment project**
Aldama Foundation
Lord and Lady Aldington
Mrs Allen-Huxley
Joan and Robin Alvarez
The Anson Charitable Trust
Artists Collecting Society
Veronica and Lars Bane
Sir David and Lady Bell
Ms Linda Bennett and Mr Philip
  Harley
Charlotte Bonham-Carter
  Charitable Trust
William Brake Trust
The Deborah Loeb Brice
  Foundation
The Consuelo and Anthony Brooke
  Charitable Trust
Garvin and Steffanie Brown
Mr and Mrs John Burns
Peter and Sally Cadbury
Carew Pole Charitable Trust
Dr Edmund Carter
Mr Richard Chang
Sir Trevor and Lady Susan Chinn
Mr and Mrs Jonathan Clarke
Mr Andrés Clase
The John S Cohen Foundation
Ms Elizabeth Crain
Crankstart
Ina De and James Spicer
The Roger De Haan Charitable
  Trust
Sir Harry Djanogly
The Gilbert and Eileen Edgar
  Foundation
The John Ellerman Foundation
Mr Richard Elman
The Lord Faringdon Charitable
  Trust
Mr and Mrs Stephen Fitzgerald
Genesis Foundation
Mr Thomas Gibson
The Golden Bottle Trust
Nicholas and Judith Goodison's
  Charitable Settlement
Antony Gormley and Vicken
  Parsons
Mr Stephen Gosztony
The late Sir Ronald Grierson
Sir Nicholas Grimshaw CBE PPRA
Fiona and Peter Hare
Mr and Mrs Julian Heslop
Holbeck Charitable Trust
The Charles Michael Holloway
  Charitable Trust
Mr and Mrs Jeremy Hosking
Huo Family Foundation (UK)
Harry Hymar and family
The Inchcape Foundation

Japanese Committee of Honour
  of The Royal Academy of Arts
Chantal Joffe RA
Alistair D K Johnston CMG FCA
Mr Ivan Katzen
Christopher Le Brun PPRA and
  Charlotte Verity
The David Lean Foundation
The Lennox and Wyfold
  Foundation
Mr Nelson Leong
Mr and Mrs Mark Loveday
Dr Lee MacCormick Edwards
  Charitable Foundation
Mr and Mrs Donald Main
Mr Javad and Mrs Narmina
  Marandi
J P Marland Charitable Trust
The late Mr Minoru Mori Hon KBE
  and Mrs Mori
Lady Alison Myners
Normanby Charitable Trust
HRH Princess Marie-Chantal of
  Greece
Mr Charles Outhwaite
Yana and Stephen Peel
Grayson Perry CBE RA
Simon and Midge Palley
John H Pattisson
The Pilgrim Trust
Mr and Mrs Maurice Pinto
The Polonsky Foundation
Mrs Tineke Pugh
Red Butterfly Foundation
The Estate of the late Mr Ivor Rey
Peter Rippon
Sir Simon and Victoria, Lady
  Robey OBE
Richard and Ruth Rogers
The Rose Foundation
Sir Paul and Lady Ruddock
Mr Wafic Rida Saïd
The Basil Samuel Charitable Trust
Mrs Coral Samuel CBE
Edwina Sassoon
Guy Senior, in memory of
  Brian and Mary Senior, Friends
  of the RA
Louisa Service OBE
David and Sophie Shalit
Archie Sherman Charitable Trust
Mr Brian Smith
Mr Christopher Smith
Sir Paul and Lady Smith
The South Square Trust
Mr and Mrs Roger Staton
Sir Hugh and Lady Stevenson
The Nina and Roger Stewart
  Charitable Trust
The late Sir David Tang KBE
Tavolozza Foundation
Tileyard Studios
Julian and Louisa Treger
Celia Walker Art Foundation
Martin and Anja Weiss
Sian and Matthew Westerman
Chris Wilkinson OBE RA and Diana
  Wilkinson
Mr Peter Williams
Ivor and Caroline Windsor
The Harold Hyam Wingate
  Foundation
Manuela and Iwan Wirth
The Lennox and Wyfold
  Foundation
Rose Wylie RA
David Zwirner
Mr Yuzo Yagi

**Major benefactors towards
redeveloping the RA schools**
Julia and Hans Rausing

Dunard Fund
The Band Trust
Adrian Cheng
Lady Alison Deighton
The Garfield Weston Foundation
Mrs Gabrielle Jungels-Winkler
Nicolette and Frederick Kwok
The Mead Family Foundation
Milner Educational Trust
The Estate of the late Miss
  Constance-Anne Parker
Jake and Hélène Marie Shafran
Sir Siegmund Warburg's Voluntary
  Settlement

**Major benefactors of the RA
schools endowment fund**
Dunard Fund
Ronald and Rita McAulay
Chenevière Travel Award
Sir Roger de Grey Memorial Fund
The Eranda Rothschild Foundation
Peter Greenham Fund
E Vincent Harris Fund
J Heritage Peters Maintenance
  Fund
Ivor Rey Scholarship Fund
Schools Portfolio Fund
The Estate of the late Mrs Pauline
  Sitwell
Starr Fund
Patricia Turner Award
Vandaleur

Benefactors of the RA schools
Archie Sherman Trust
Artists Collecting Society
Charlotte Bonham-Carter
  Charitable Trust
William Brake Trust
John S Cohen Foundation
Ron Dennis
Dreamchasing
The Gilbert and Eileen Edgar
  Foundation
Epson
The Eranda Rothschild Foundation
Peter Greenham Fund
Holbeck Charitable Trust
The Charles Michael Holloway
  Charitable Trust
Leverhulme Trust
The Normanby Charitable Trust
Mr and Mrs Mark Loveday
Mr Nelson Leong
The Maccabaeans
The Machin Foundation
Dr Lee MacCormick Edwards
  Charitable Foundation
The Batia and Idan Ofer Family
  Foundation
Andrés Olow Clase
Christina Ong
Red Butterfly Foundation
The Estate of the late Mr Ivor Rey
Peter Rippon
The Rose Foundation
Bianca Roden
Archie Sherman Charitable Trust
David and Deborah Stileman
The South Square Trust
Sir Paul and Lady Smith
Stanley Picker Charitable Trust
The Stewarts Foundation
The Nina and Roger Stewart
  Charitable Trust
The Adrian Swire Charitable Trust
The Swire Charitable Trust
Tileyard Studios
Celia Walker Art Foundation
Mr W Galen Weston and the Hon
  Mrs Hilary Weston

The Harold Hyam Wingate
  Foundation
*and those who wish to remain
anonymous*

Patrons

Chair of RA patrons
Mr Matthew Langton

International circle
Mrs Niloufar Bakhtiar-Bakhtiar
Mr Lars Bane
Lady Alison Deighton
Ms Ida Levine
Mr Nick Loup
Mr Thaddaeus Ropac
Yukiko and Anders U Schroeder
Ms Chizuko Yashiro
Mr and Mrs Basil Zirinis
*and those who wish to remain
anonymous*

Platinum patrons
Paul Baines
Mr Christopher Bake
The Deborah Loeb Brice
  Foundation
Hugo Eddis
Mr Stephen Gosztony
Mr Jim Grover
Charles and Kaaren Hale
Mr Yan Huo
Mrs Bianca Roden
Mr Howard Shore
Mr Peter Williams
*and those who wish to remain
anonymous*

Gold patrons
Mr Stephen Allcock
Joan and Robin Alvarez
Ms Vanessa Aubry
Sir Francis Brooke Bt
Mr Thomas Cantwell
Ms Lisa Carrodus
Christopher and Alex Courage
Mrs Kate de Rothschild
Swag and Nupur Ganguly
Mr Stephen E Griggs
Mrs Elizabeth Hosking
Dame Vivian Hunt
Mr Christopher Kneale
Ms Maxine Kohn
Sir Sydney Lipworth QC and Lady
  Lipworth
Mr William Loschert
Mr Nicholas Maclean
Scott and Laura Malkin
Mr Stephen Marquardt
Simon and Sabi North
Miss Asta Paulauskaite
Yana and Stephen Peel
Paulo and Caroline Pereira
Melanie Rademacher
The Lady Renwick of Clifton
Tania Rotherwick
Mr Richard Simmons CBE
Mr Tim Smith
Mr Kevin Sneader and Ms Amy
  Muntner
Jane Spack
Raksha Sriram
Mr Michael Stiff
David Stileman
Robert Suss
Rebecca Taylor
Frederick and Kathryn Uhde
Countess Cornelia Von Rittberg
Erica Wax
Mrs Janet Winslow
Manuela and Iwan Wirth